INSIDE STORIES

INSIDE STORIES

Wisdom and hope for changing worlds

A resource for classrooms and workshops

Angela Wood and Robin Richardson

Trentham Books

First published in 1992 by Trentham Books Limited

Trentham Books Limited
Westview House,
734 London Road,
Oakhill, Stoke-on-Trent,
Staffordshire ST4 5NP

British Cataloguing in Publication Data
A catalogue record for this book is available from the British Library.

ISBN 0 948080 68 X

Cover illustration by Shirley Harris.

Designed and typeset by Trentham Print Design Ltd, Chester
and printed in Great Britain by Bemrose Shafron Ltd, Chester.

Contents

To all insiders
and
all outsiders

1
The Story So Far

Summary

The Table of Contents is a kind of preliminary map, to show how this book holds together.

First, on pages 7-20, there are some stories about storytelling and storylistening, to introduce a number of key ideas about the nature and importance of narrative, and about the importance of narrative in human affairs. Next, some principles and reflections about storytelling and narrative are set out briefly on pages 21-26. Amongst other things, this section of the book serves as an introduction to the fifty stories which are to follow.

Next, on pages 35-108, there is the heart of the book: a collection of fifty stories for you to adapt and use as you wish. They have been arranged to suggest a sequence of fundamental experiences on the journey from birth to death. They show people entering, challenging and enlarging the cultural traditions into which they are born; and therefore working and organising, loving and struggling, reflecting and transforming. The stories are grouped under seven main headings, corresponding to seven main stages or tasks of human development:

✪ emerging
birth, growth, parents, maturity

✪ seeking
wonderings, wanderings, quests, questions

✪ loving
family, friends, lovers, partners

✪ challenging
conflict, assertion, defiance, liberation

✪ organising
creating, building, managing, leading

✪ reflecting
review, recollection, meanings, wisdom

✪ transforming
mortality, endings, hope, renewal

Then on pages 109-120 there is a series of suggestions of practical ways in which you can help your learners to listen to stories, and to interpret and learn from them, and to create and develop their own. On pages 123-154 there are notes on each of the stories in this book, with information about their source, treatment, background and points for reflection.

Finally, there is an index of traditions (page 156), an index of titles (page 156), and a select bibliography (page 158).

The Palm of the Hand

Nobody, but nobody, was paying attention. Her arguments were sound, her ideas compelling, her phrasings striking. But her speech was falling on stony ground. No one was taking any interest. She paused. 'Once upon a time,' she said, starting again. Suddenly everyone was quiet, everyone was listening.

'Once upon a time, the Prime Minister of India went for a walk with a swallow and an eel.' She had them all now, she knew, in the palm of her hand.

Word of Mouth

It was Aesop, in Ancient Greece, who first wrote down a version of the story on the previous page. Aesop knew, and countless millions of storytellers over the centuries have known, that people pay attention to you when you tell them a story. People love stories.

Many stories contain the features which are present in Aesop's tale of the speaker. First, there is a problem — there is a character who doesn't know at the start of the story what to do. Second, there is some sort of a resolution — the character finds out what to do, or anyway the listener does.

Further, stories frequently contain the two main ingredients of Aesop's unfinished story-within-a-story of the prime minister, the swallow and the eel: there is some sort of mystery or puzzle in the story's situation, and the problem to be solved is then for the listener as well as for the characters. For example, as in Aesop's story here, two or more people, events or outlooks may be brought together in an unpredictable and surprising encounter.

Also, however, we expect that there will be reasons, consequences, meanings. We do not know why the prime minister, the swallow and the eel set out on a journey together, nor why they happened to be together in the first place. We listen to the story in order to find these things out, and in the belief that indeed a meaning is going to be found. We crave stories because we crave meanings.

We make and share stories with each other in many different ways — through all sorts of printed media, very obviously, and through films, pictures, signs and symbols. But most importantly of all, we share stories by word of mouth.

This Book's Uses

This book is about oral traditions of storytelling and storylistening. It is intended in particular for teachers in schools, and is both a reflection and a resource:

❂ *Reflection*

As a reflection of oral traditions, the book recalls some of the knowledge, experience and expertise of millions of teachers all over the world, both in the present and in the past; and how they use stories, in order to instruct and to inform, and to enlighten and educate.

❂ *Resource*

As a resource, the book is a support and a guide for all who wish to enter into oral traditions of storytelling more fully, and who wish to take and unfold the traditions further.

You are likely to find the book useful if:

❂ *Religious education*

You are a teacher of religious education in a secondary school, and you wish your pupils to become more familiar with the role, nature and functions of narrative in the history and development of the world's religious faiths, and in the daily lives and imaginations of religious believers. Perhaps in particular you wish to teach through stories how different religious traditions view the successive stages of human life, and the fundamental experiences which all people meet on their journey from birth to death.

❂ *Personal and Social Education*

You are a teacher of personal and social education in a secondary school, and you wish to use fables, parables and wisdom tales in order to raise and explore questions of morality and principle in everyday life.

❂ *English*

You are a teacher of English in a secondary school, and you wish to add to the range of stories, genres and narrative styles which you already use, and to your repertoire of practical ways of exploring stories in the classroom.

❂ *Assemblies*

You sometimes have responsibility for organising an assembly or act of collective worship, and wish to use symbolic stories and parables in order to stimulate curiosity and reflection.

The Title

A word about the book's title. It has at least four different meanings. Between them, these four meanings give a good idea of the book's main concerns:

1) What insiders know

It is through knowing a community's or culture's stories that you get to know it from within. It may be that you wish to know your own tradition better. Or perhaps your aim is to deepen your knowledge of another tradition. Either way you can enter through the tradition's stories; it is these which give you the low-down, the inside knowledge. Stories give you the keys, the code, they let you in and show you round.

2) Internalising

In order to understand a story you have to get inside it, so to speak. This may involve visualising vividly the events which are described. Certainly it involves paying close attention. Only then can you find the meaning which the storyteller has embodied and encoded, and only then can you make the meaning your own.

3) Inside, there are stories

Inside each individual, and inside each community, society and culture, there are stories: not raw material, unprocessed, but carefully constructed and patterned narratives and accounts. People construct and develop the stories which are inside themselves by talking and reflecting about events with others. And by listening to the stories which others tell, from within their lives.

4) Stories about the inside

The stories in this book are about people's inner lives — their loves, strengths and resolutions, and their anxieties, hurts and yearnings, as they move through life.

2
Story Stories

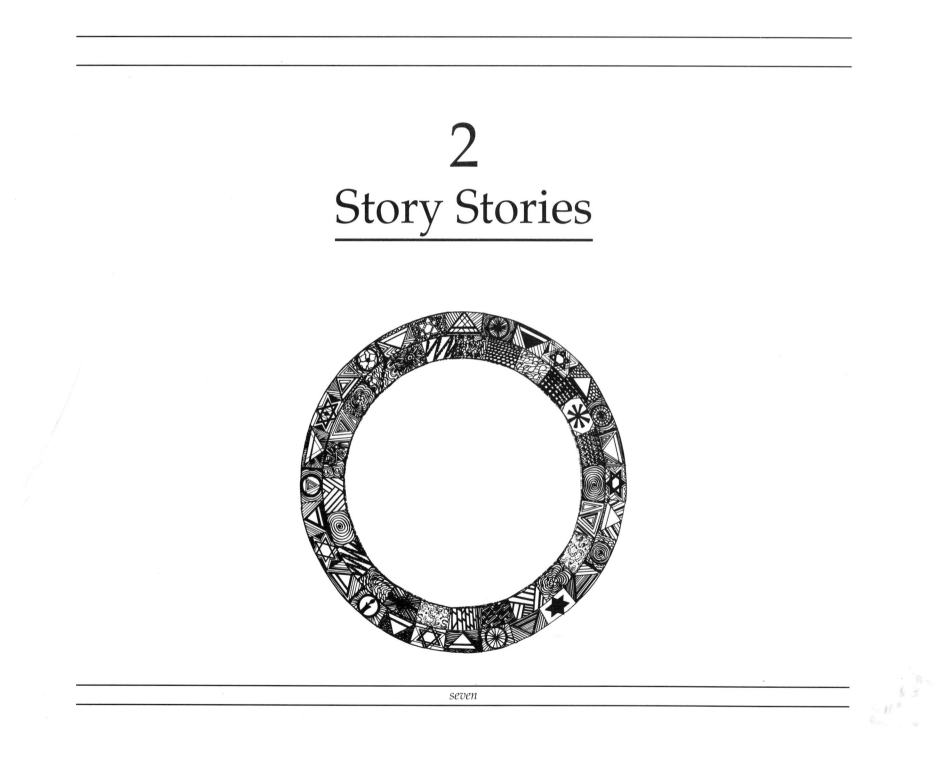

Story Stories

On pages 9-20 there are ten stories about the nature and importance of stories. They are as follows:

In the section entitled Once Upon a Time...., starting on page 125, there are notes about these ten 'story stories', referring to their backgrounds, origins and treatments, and to the reflections which they prompt or invite.

What Sort of a Person?

Once upon a time there were three people in a balloon, floating gracefully over the land. One was a senior police officer. She had, she reckoned, seen everything in the course of her career. She knew all of humankind's crimes, cowardice and foolishness: there was nothing in human nature which could surprise her. The second was a famous psychologist. He knew intimately the inside of people's minds and hearts: everything that makes people tick. The third was a small child.

As they journeyed high· above the countryside in their balloon, they realised that they had strayed from their intended route. They resolved to bring the balloon down close to the land and to ask someone on the ground where they were.

They came down towards the land and saw someone beneath them in a field. 'Where are we?' shouted the police officer and the psychologist. 'You're in a balloon,' shouted back the person standing in the field.

The police officer and the psychologist looked at each other in amazement. 'What sort of a person could that be?' asked the one. 'Never, never in all my long experience of human nature,' said the other, 'have I come across someone like that. What sort of a person could it be?'

'Well,' said the small child, 'I have actually met quite a lot of adults like that in the course of my life. But I do know one thing. That person cannot be a storyteller.'

'Oh?' said the others. 'How can you tell that?'

'There are three reasons,' said the child. 'First, what the person said was completely obvious. Second, it was completely uninteresting. Third, it was completely useless. Yes definitely, that person cannot be a storyteller.'

Because of the Seed muslim

Once in Baghdad there was a very good sultan, much loved and admired by all his subjects. He was kind and helpful, always energetic and caring, and above all he was just.

Parents are at their best when they are both caring and just, and both kind and strong, and so are teachers and bosses and rulers of all kinds, and in all places and at all times.

How had it come about that the sultan in Baghdad was so wise? What was his secret? Had he been born like this? Was it the way he had been brought up?

The people wondered and asked each other. One day a very wise old storyteller came to Baghdad, and the people asked her opinion. Had the sultan been born caring and just, and kind and strong, or was it the way he had been brought up? Or was it just luck?

'I don't know,' replied the wise old storyteller, 'but I will tell you this. I was here in Baghdad when he was born, and I was invited to the banquet which his father gave to celebrate his birth. All the nobles of Baghdad were there, and they brought a great mass of very expensive presents, in particular piles and heaps of jewels and rare coins.

'I was poor then as I am also poor now, and I could not give the baby any jewels. But what I did do was to give him stories.

All through his childhood and teenage years I used to visit him at his parents' mansion, and tell him stories.'

'What were your stories about?' asked the people.

'They were stories about people on journeys, and about people asking questions and searching for answers. When people in my stories are brave, and go on and on journeying and searching, the most wonderful things happen to them. Sometimes...'

'Yes?' asked the people. 'Sometimes?'

'Sometimes in my stories it's as if people come close to God. Not that I ever use the word God, I dare not name him, I dare not think as big as that.'

'Are you telling the truth?' asked the people. 'Or is this just another of your stories?'

The storyteller smiled, but did not answer.

On the monument which his people made when the good sultan died, there were these few simple words, very carefully and very beautifully crafted:

IT WAS BECAUSE OF THE SEED SOWN BY THE TALES.

Forest, Fire and Prayer Jewish.

Whenever Rabbi Baal Shem Tov realised that the Jewish community was in danger, he would plead to God on their behalf: he would go to a certain place in the forest to meditate, light a fire and say a special prayer. Every time, a miracle would happen and the disaster would be avoided.

Whenever the famous Magid of Mezeritch realised that the Jewish community was in danger, he would plead to God on their behalf: he would go to a certain place in the forest to meditate and pray, and he would say, 'I do not know how to light the fire, but I am able to say the prayer and surely this will be sufficient!' It was sufficient! Every time, a miracle would happen and the disaster would be avoided.

Whenever Rabbi Moshe-Leib of Sasov realised that the Jewish community was in danger, he would plead to God on their behalf: he would go to a certain place in the forest to meditate, saying, 'I do not know how to light the fire, and I do not know the prayer; but I do know the place, and surely this will be sufficient.' It was sufficient! Every time, a miracle would happen and the disaster would be avoided.

Whenever Rabbi Israel of Rizhyn realised that the Jewish community was in danger, he would plead to God on their behalf. Sitting in his armchair with his head in his hands, he spoke to God: 'I am unable to light the fire, and I do not know the prayer; I cannot even find the place in the forest. All I can do is tell this story and surely this will be sufficient.' And it was sufficient.

Nights and Mornings   muslim

The king hated life. His food had no taste or zest. There was no spring in his stride or light in his eyes; no newness in his mornings, no contentment or rest in his nights. He was disgusted by women, and incapable of love.

He was all-powerful. It was his privilege that he could throw his weight around, and no one could stop him. To get his revenge on life, he furiously decided that he would marry lots and lots of women, one after another, and that he would have each of them beheaded at dawn on the day after the wedding. And this he began to do. He married a young girl, spent one night with her, and then had her beheaded at dawn the following morning. He did this many times. He could throw his weight around, and throw it around he did.

One day he married Shahrazad. She was clever and shrewd, and absolutely determined to save her life. She had no hesitation about using guile and deceit. She was entirely ready, for example, to pretend to the king that she liked him, loved him, cared for him. As they lay together on their wedding night she said, 'My dearest, I want to tell you a story.' And she began, 'In the name of Allah, the Compassionate, the Merciful, Creator of the Universe, who has raised the heavens without pillars. Once upon a time there was. . .' It was a fascinating story, and the king listened intently to the events and rhythms,

the patterns and the unfolding. But before she got to the end of the story, Shahrazad pretended to go to sleep. She lay there in the king's arms, and there was nothing he could do to wake her. So he waited patiently through the night, anxious and excited to hear the rest of the story. There was no question of having her beheaded at dawn. The following morning Shahrazad told the story through to the end.

That evening, the same thing happened. 'In the name of Allah, the Compassionate, the Merciful, Creator of the Universe, who has raised the heavens without pillars. Once upon a time there was. . .' She began telling a fascinating story, and the king listened enthralled to the events and rhythms, the patterns and unfolding. But before getting to the end she pretended to fall asleep, and the king had to wait with anxiety and excitement till the following morning for the story's ending. There was no question of having her beheaded at dawn.

And so it went on, night after night, morning after morning. Shahrazad told 1000 stories altogether, beginning on one thousand nights, and ending on one thousand mornings. There were the stories of Sinbad, Aladdin and Ali Baba; the story of the great caliph Haroun al Rashid; stories about a fisherman and a sultan, a pomegranate in the sea, a magic horse: exactly one thousand stories altogether. Each began in the same way: 'In the name of Allah, the Compassionate, the Merciful, Creator of the Universe, who has raised the heavens without pillars. Once upon a time there was. . .'

By now, after one thousand nights and one thousand mornings, both Shahrazad and the king had changed. He no longer hated life. Food was delightful to him, he loved walking and seeing, everything in the world seemed to fit together for him in a glorious pattern. He respected and admired, and he cared for, all the people whom he knew. He ruled his country with wisdom and justice. He loved Shahrazad.

And Shahrazad was no longer lying when she said to him, 'my dearest. . .' At some stage during the 1000 nights she had fallen in love with him. When exactly it had happened she did not know. All she knew was that now she loved him, dearly.

It was on the one thousandth and first night that she told him this, and that he in return declared his love to her. The story began as all others had done: 'In the name of Allah, the Compassionate, the Merciful, Creator of the Universe, who has raised the heavens without pillars. Once upon a time there was. . .' But on that night she told her story through to the end.

Your Own Story

A young man called one day on the Teacher. 'I am seeking happiness,' he said, 'and am prepared to study hard. Will you please recommend some books for me to read?'

'You need learning and you need wisdom, these two separate things.' That's what the Teacher said first, by way of reply.

'You get learning by listening to stories and reading books, and talking and thinking about them. Yes, I can recommend some books. But it's more important to listen to stories than to read them. Hearing and listening, I assure you, are more important than reading and studying.'

'And wisdom?' asked the young man. 'How do I attain wisdom?'

' You get wisdom, ' replied the Teacher, ' by listening to your own story. You are a book, and you have to read and study the book which is you.'

The young man looked puzzled.

'And it's difficult, very difficult,' continued the Teacher. 'Because every day there's a new page, and every moment there's a new word, in the book which is you.'

Put to the Test Muslim

I've had my times — and I can't say I've ever been bored. But it was when the King told me that he wanted to become a holy man, just like me, that things really began to get exciting. 'Lead me in the path of wisdom, and guide me in the mystic way,' he said. He'd been very successful as a king, no doubt about it. He had become very wealthy, and conquered many lands. So for him the sky was the limit.

The trouble is that success as a king and success as a holy man are not exactly the same thing, to put it mildly. The question was: how could I get him to see this without causing offence?

'Forgive me, Your Majesty,' I says to him. 'But in my humble opinion, and with the deepest respect, I do not think you were born to be a holy man. I mean, the test you would have to take is very strict and difficult — not at all suitable for someone of such noble birth as yourself.'

'Away with such thoughts! You think that I'll fail the test, don't you? The desert will turn to ice before I fail, let me tell you that! Have I not subdued all our enemies, amassed great wealth and conquered many lands? Surely you don't really think that a simple test to be a holy man will bother me!'

So I told him, 'Your Majesty, it would hurt me more than I can say to see you fail . . . but I can see how determined you are and I cannot stand in your way. If you fail, it must be because you have let yourself down, not because I shut you out.'

It was then we struck a deal: he would take his test in an open court. That way anybody and everybody could see what a stupid thing it is to mess around, and nobody would waste my time with similar ideas again. At least that way I would get something out of it, and the king would be happy because he would get a chance to prove himself.

My next problem was what sort of a test to set him: I didn't want him to look an absolute fool but I did want to wrap the whole thing up once and for all. Then the idea struck me. . . I explained to him: 'All you have to do is reply 'I believe you' to whatever I say. Okay? Here we go. A thousand years ago, I went to heaven.'

'I believe you,' replied the king.

'I shall never grow old like other people, and I shall never die.'

'I believe you.'

'I have been to places where the rain falls upwards and the sun is cold and people are smaller than ants.'

'I believe you.'

This was going very nicely. 'I have taught people who didn't want to be taught, and I have failed to teach people who did want to be taught. When I was lying people thought I was telling the truth and when I was telling the truth they thought I was lying. . .'

'I believe you,' replied the king again.

'Once I even met your parents, Your Majesty, and I found that they were liars and cheats.'

'What?' raged the king. 'I don't believe a word of it!'

Naked Truth

Truth was having a really lousy time. He was covering a whole lot of space but he was strictly non-cool and no one seemed to dig him. He wanted to do his own thing but when guys saw him coming, they took a dive. He just couldn't cope. It was doing his ego no good. Eventually, he freaked out.

'What's your trouble, man?' asked parable. She was dressed up to the nines and on a real high. 'You look like you're having a bomber.'

'I don't get it,'said Truth. 'Whenever I come on, I get the push off the whole time. Is there something they're not telling me?'

'You're a far out dude, that's what! The way you look, it's a heavy scene. You've got nothing on, like you're some kind of weirdo. Who can handle you like that? You need to smarten up your act a little. Use some of my gear — it'll get you a piece of the action!'

'Nah, it looks great on you but it's not my speed. Why can't they take me the way I am?'

'Look, just stop asking dumb questions. They can't, OK. Right now, you can't even take yourself the way you are. D'you think I never felt like that? Sure I did — we're the same underneath — but I try to make something of my life and feel good about myself.'

So Truth gave it a go. And his life took an up.

The Book

'Serapion, Serapion, what have you done?' said the master. 'The other monks tell me that you have sold your Gospel and bought food for the hungry. Such a precious book of Our Lord's life —
how could you do it?'

'How could I not do it?' Serapion replied. 'I have sold the book which tells me to sell all that we have to give to the poor.'

Seed Progress Report

Ladies and gentlemen,

I begin my report to the company's shareholders this year by giving an account of the launch and marketing of our major new software package, the SEED desktop publishing system. In addition to the normal press, radio and TV advertising, and personalised mail shots to 5000 selected companies, institutions and organisations, we conducted an intensive publicity campaign in four specific towns.

It is about the publicity campaign in four specific towns that I wish to report to you in some detail. I think you will find the results very fascinating, and that they provide much food for thought. For the sake of convenience, I shall call these four towns Appatheaton, Brashbury, Cooloffham and Deapchangeley. At first sight they are extremely similar to each other, for example in terms of size, prosperity, social mix, ethnic composition, age structure, range of occupations, political voting patterns, amenities and transport, and so on. You would think that if SEED were to succeed in one of these towns then it would be bound to succeed in all the others also. However, each town reacted to SEED in its own very distinctive way. This is what I wish to tell you about.

(A) **Appatheaton**

In Appatheaton, to put the matter bluntly, our campaign was a disaster. Virtually no one in the town took the slightest interest. SEED, as I am sure everyone here today knows, is a very versatile publishing package indeed, and has the potential of being able to transform people's lives, in a whole range of fascinating and creative ways. In Appatheaton, however, we were totally unable to get any reasonable sales.

(B) **Brashbury**

In Brashbury we were more successful. Indeed, sales were very satisfactory indeed. A large number of firms and organisations purchased our product. The sad and disturbing fact, however, is that although lots of people acquired SEED, and although in doing so they spent quite large sums of money, they have not actually used it! SEED has had no discernible impact on them.

(C) Cooloffham

In Cooloffham actual sales were not as good as in Brashbury. But at least it was gratifying to see companies which acquired SEED did immediately start using the package, and were extremely enthusiastic. We have received an impressive number of glowing letters. Yet sadly, I have to admit to you, once the initial euphoria had died down SEED was basically tidied away. The position now, a few months after the marketing campaign, is that SEED is no more used in Cooloffham than it is in Brashbury.

(D) Deapchangeley

Deapchangeley, I am happy to report to you, was a real success story. Sales have increased steadily since the launch, and our profits are very pleasing indeed. More importantly — much more importantly — SEED is being widely used throughout the town, and it is transforming people's lives. There has been an explosion of community newspapers, and of company news-letters and bulletins. There are several small publishing houses, producing stories, auto-biography and poetry written by local people. There are vigorous new networks and relation-ships throughout the town, and very large numbers of people are gaining fulfilment through writing, printing, publishing and sharing their ideas and their stories. SEED stands, you recall, for SENSITIVITY, ENLIGHT-ENMENT, EMPOWERMENT and DELIGHT. It has cer-tainly lived up to its name in Deapchangeley.

We are — I will be frank with you — puzzled by these four differing responses to the same package. For I repeat and emphasise, the four towns are apparently very similar to each other. We are very keen to have light thrown on this matter, if at all possible. We wonder, therefore, whether any of you here today have any comments or suggestions? Have you ever heard a similar story?

The Real Thing

He ached for her day and night. He couldn't sleep, couldn't eat — could hardly even think! Nothing made sense without her and he knew he could would never feel right until they were together. How he longed for her to know the secrets of his heart and to share his love, but how could be begin to tell her?

Not a day passed that he did not write to her, though words did not come easily. Sometimes his letters were full of passion; sometimes soft words fell gently on the page. Some he laboured over for hours; some flew spontaneously from his pen. One he scribbled on the back of a packet; one was stored on disk — and never printed . . . And none was ever sent!

Before long, boxes of unsent letters filled his room. The pain of life without her was unbearable and he knew it must end soon.

It was more than he had ever dreamed when she said she would meet him. Just waiting for her made him tingle. The moment came when he saw her face to face, gazed deep into her eyes and all the love he felt welled up inside him. But words failed him altogether now, and so he took from his pocket bundles of letters he hadn't dare send. One by one he read them to her, with full expression and deep meaning: they told her stories about how much he wanted to touch her, to feel her close to him, to be one with her . . .

The hours wore on until finally she snapped and blurted out, 'I don't get you! You're reading out all these letters in which you've written about, you know, how you fancy me and how you want to get me on my own and that . . . But you're not doing anything, not even saying anything: I am real, you know!'

She leant forward to kiss him.

3
The World of Story

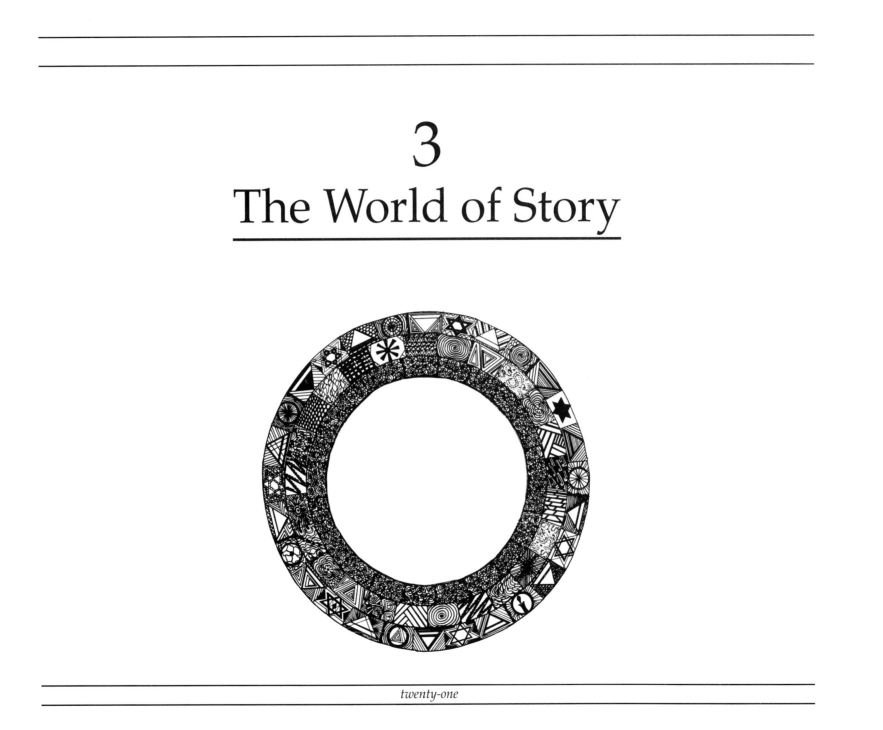

Contents of this chapter

Please note: the teachings and themes are summarised on page 28, and then each is explained in further detail on pages 29-33.

The centrality of narrative

What's new? What did you do today? What have you done since we last met? How's life treating you? What's happened?

In these ways, and in many others, we ask to be told stories. And in answer to such questions, we all tell stories through the day, and every day. We turn to TV and to newspapers and magazines, in order to take in stories, and to chat about them and chew on them, discuss and digest them. Much of our conversation each day, particularly our conversation with the people we are closest to and care most about, is based around stories. Human beings, it can be said, are animals who tell, listen to, discuss, dwell on, are moved by, stories.

The stories on pages 9-20 recall some of the fundamental features of narrative and storytelling. The child in the balloon (*What Sort of a Person?*) reminds us that stories have to be intriguing and interesting as distinct from obvious and banal, and that they are in some way useful and helpful to us even though they may not be literally 'true'. The next two tales show some of the practical uses of storytelling. The ruler in *Because of the Seed* is wise and kind and strong, it is said, because of the stories which he was told when he was a child. Also the ruler in *Nights and Mornings* is changed by caring and wondering about stories, and storytelling and storylistening are the bonds which enable the two main characters to fall in love with each other.

Religious faith and community solidarity are nurtured, sustained and strengthened by stories, as shown in the tale of the rabbis in *Forest, Fire and Prayer,* and stories do this in part by pointing beyond themselves through paradox and irony, as in *The Book*. *Naked Truth* emphasises the importance of symbolism, fantasy and metaphor in storytelling, but *Put to the Test* shows that the fantasies in stories nevertheless have to be tested against the realities of experience and everyday living. Similarly *The Real Thing* notes the distinction between stories and reality, and warns against confusing the two.

Your Own Story introduces the idea that each person's life is a kind of story, with a beginning, a middle and an end, and suggests that it is in order to get a grip on our life-stories as wholes that we turn to the legends, myths and fables of tradition. *Seed Progress Report*, based on a famous parable about differing responses to the same message, recalls that stories are not always understood and acted upon; it recalls also, however, that they have the potential to nurture, as it is said, 'sensitivity, enlightenment, empowerment and delight'.

Story in everyday life

In order to understand the importance of the great oral traditions, it is valuable to reflect first on the role and importance of story and narrative in our everyday conversations and encounters. There are three main points in this regard:

⚙ **To understand**

We tell stories to each other, in our everyday chat and conversation about events close to us, in order to understand why things happen, and how events are connected with each other. Our experience of life isn't just one inconsequential thing after another, stories say, but is full of threads, links, causes, consequences.

⚙ **To manage**

We tell stories to get a grip on life. That is, in order to feel clearer about how we and others ought to behave and feel. Stories provide tips, guidance, warnings and suggestions.

⚙ **To share**

A consequence of swapping stories with others is that we bind ourselves more closely to them. For in building and sharing narratives, we are also building up shared agendas, values and intentions.

But it is not only that our lives are made up of thousands and thousands of stories — countless episodes and events, most of them ephemeral and small-scale, but some of them truly traumatic and life-changing. Also, each of us has a single story, or biography. There is my birth, on that day, in that place, for that mother, into that household, family, setting, community, culture. There has been, since my birth, my own personal chain of events. Ahead of me, my own unique journey will unwind. One day, there will be my one and only death. I wish and need to make sense of the overall narrative of my life, with its unique beginning and unique end, as well as of the myriad of separate parts.

Story in education

These brief reflections on the role of story in everyday and personal life are relevant to the role of traditional stories in education. When we as adults tell stories to the young, whether at school or in the home or elsewhere, we are doing four main things, either actually or potentially:

✪ **making sense**
we are helping them to make sense of their own experience of life — both their ephemeral and small-scale experiences and also their overall life-story;

✪ **developing skill**
we are helping them to become more effective as storytelling and storylistening creatures themselves, for we are providing models for them to imitate;

✪ **belonging**
we are introducing them to the heritage and traditions to which they have been born, so that they may have a sense of belonging to a community, and of being supported by a community — for our stories are about shared values and meanings, shared beliefs and insights, and shared agendas and goals;

✪ **renewing**
we are enabling culture and our community not only to be transmitted and maintained but also to be questioned, renewed, improved and developed.

Story in religion

Just as each individual life consists of many different episodes yet also has the shape of a single story, so also does a religious tradition have two main aspects. On the one hand, there are hundreds of separate stories — each religion has a store of fables, parables and cautionary tales; chronicles about heroes, martyrs, teachers and gurus; myths and legends; and histories, memories and accounts of events. On the other, there is the religion's single story, or Story: its distinctive account of how and why the universe came into existence, and its distinctive model of the good life to be lived by each individual.

It follows that if you wish to get to know a religious tradition better — whether as an insider or as an outsider — then the most valuable thing for you to do is to go inside the tradition's stories, and its Story. You need to know what happens in the stories, and in the Story, and even more importantly you need to know the meanings and connections — the ways in which narrative in the tradition casts light and gives guidance in the daily lives and life-stories of believers.

Teachings and Themes

At the start of many of the stories in this book there is a situation of injustice: someone, or a group of people, is suffering distress through absolutely no fault of their own. The basic story-line is then about how they respond to the injustice, and attempt to change not only the external situation but also, perhaps, their own feelings and understandings.

In certain of the stories the initial injustice is caused by the cruelty, callousness or malice of human beings. This is the case with the two stories set in concentration camps, *The Night We Cried* and *Hanging on for Life*, with the story of Draupadi in *Draupadi's Prayer*, with Guru Hargobind in *Speaking to the Emperor*, and — though exactly what has happened is not specified — with the woman in *The Door*. In other stories the injustice is caused by a curse, symbolising blind fate, as in *Savitri*, or by ill fortune, as in *Thrown to the World* and *In Search of a Cure*. Other examples of oppression include the situations of the main characters in *The Stonecutter* and *Paradise Gardens*, both of whom feel trapped by the chores of their everyday life, and of the rulers in *Standing Up and Sitting Down* and *Nights and Mornings*, both of whom obtain no satisfaction from their positions of leadership and responsibility. The woman in *That Dying Feeling* is faced with the injustice, as she sees it, of her own mortality and awareness of endings and loss. The young woman in *Two Kinds of Idiot is* harassed and threatened by a male-dominated world, both in her leisure time and at work.

How to respond to a situation of real or imagined injustice and unfairness? The traditional wisdom expressed in stories seldom if ever suggests that there is a single, unambiguously correct solution or a universally effective strategy. It does often provide, however, warnings against approaches and strategies which are basically unreliable and unhelpful. For example, it is emphatic in its warnings against fatalism and reliance on magical solutions, and in warnings against putting your trust in the pursuit of wealth, power and control. And it often seems to suggest that it can be more important to experience ambiguities, contradictions and tensions, and to live with them, than to try either to solve them or to avoid them.

The content of traditional wisdom is of course not easily summarised. But at the risk of the very kind of over-simplification against which it frequently and passionately warns, there seem to be ten main teachings. To an extent these qualify and correct each other, and none can stand entirely independently of the others. They are shown overleaf.

Wisdom and Hope — Teachings and Themes in the World's Stories

❶ Have faith in the past

Tradition can be trusted. A certain prudence about tradition is most certainly necessary, for there are dangers in conservatism for conservatism's sake. But basically the customs and insights we have inherited from the past, and which are treasured by our grandmothers and grandfathers, are — so to speak — innocent until proved guilty.

❷ Don't walk away

There are no easy answers or quick-fix solutions. But we human beings do have many gifts, skills and valuable qualities, and we should at least rely on these rather than on luck or magic. Definitely there is no place for passive fatalism.

❸ You can't take it with you

It's frequently tempting and 'natural', but misguided and unhelpful, to trust in material possessions or power over others. Wealth and power are mirages, alas, and have no real or lasting value.

❹ Love one another

We can and should commend love and affection between human beings, and devote a lot of energy to keeping our friendships, relationships, families, households and love affairs in good repair. Also the fabric of society needs keeping in good repair, so that love and affection between individuals and in small groups can grow and flourish.

❺ Use your head

We may take reasonable pride in human intelligence, ingenuity and imagination — and we should expect, in this connection, that society's laws and customs are created and maintained by reasonable people, and that they will, by and large, therefore work to our advantage.

❻ Love life

Life is good — the air we breathe, the sun on our faces, the vigour in our limbs and senses, our sexuality, our food and drink, work and play.

❼ Keep going

We should prize dignity, perserverance and courage, and our capacity to keep on hoping.

❽ Look with new eyes

It's important to develop new ways of seeing, and to see connections between apparently unrelated happenings and details, and see events and trends in perspective.

❾ Let go

We need to value acceptance and serenity — the capacity to live humbly with constraints and limits, and with ambiguity and uncertainty.

❿ And never stop telling stories

Truth can often only be expressed through paradox, imagery and metaphor, and often indeed only through an ambiguous and paradoxical story.

These ten teachings are described in further detail on pages 29-33, and in each instance there are references to stories in this book which explain and illustrate the ideas further.

❶ Have faith in the past

Traditional stories commend openness to new experience, but also often emphasise the value of tradition itself: the wisdom in treasures which we have inherited from the past, and the danger of frittering them away. Over and over again, they commend the insights, ideas and achievements of previous generations, and their legacy of precious traditions and customs.

Many stories present this theme entirely directly, as for example *Standing Up and Sitting Down*. Most present it also indirectly, by themselves being an embodiment of traditional wisdom. It is of course no accident, in this connection, that in all cultures and communities the most respected storytellers are the old and elderly, the grandmothers and grandfathers of the present generation, as in *Thrown to the World*. It is in stories rather than in rituals or in beliefs that traditional wisdom is stored, as in *Forest, Fire and Prayer*.

The wisdom of the past is explicitly referred to in *Hush My Baby*, the story set in a modern childcare clinic. In *Say No More* and *The Precious Stone* there are representatives of traditional wisdom and imagery of wealth and treasure to emphasise the values of tradition. The rabbi in *Hanging On For Life* trusts the faith handed down to him by his ancestors, and Kevin in *Slender Threads* devotes time to the study of sacred writings.

❷ Don't walk away

The first speaker in *Thrown to the World* holds a stone, and advocates resignation to whatever fate has in store. The second fingers a bracelet, and argues the case for believing in luck and magic. In many of the other stories in this book there are characters who have a fatalistic belief that there is nothing they themselves can do to alter or improve the situation in which they find themselves.

Thus, for example, the father in *In the Dark and the Day* uses a story about a magic charm to control his daughter, and the family in *Means and Ends* relies on divine intervention in the abstract rather than working through other human beings. Similarly the man in *Just the Ticket* believes that simply believing in luck will bring success, and the main character in *Say No More* thinks that there is a magical solution to his need for material possessions and a place to live. Prince Yuddhishtira in *Draupadi's Prayer* gambles everything in a game of dice, believing wrongly that sheer chance will be on his side. The mechanic in *God Willing* implies that everything depends on fate rather than on his own efforts, and it is clear that the Mother Superior in this story is opposed to resignation as an aspect of religious faith. The jokey story *Is There Anybody There?* has much the same message — belief in God, it seems to be saying, is not the same as believing in miraculous interventions when all else fails.

Other stories explore the difference between superstition and resignation, on the one hand, and mature acceptance of mystery combined with realistic reliability on human capacities for love and courage, on the other. This distinction is at the heart of *Daring to Fly*, for example, and of *In Search of a Cure, Hanging on for Life*, and *Whoever Comes This Way*.

❸ You can't take it with you

In very many stories there are characters who believe that all that is necessary in life is to have wealth, or to wield power over others. They will then be safe, they believe, from all or most kinds of ill fortune and unfairness. But traditional stories consistently show that such security is illusory, for it cannot ensure love and affection from other human beings, and cannot help people to live — and to die — with dignity and a sense of purpose.

The couple in *So Near and So Far* set out to find material treasure, and the businessman in *The Precious Stone* is concerned at the start only with material wealth. Both discover that their search is, in an important sense, misconceived. Similarly the ruler in *The Needle*, who amongst other things takes special pleasure in showing his wealth off to others, learns that there is more to life than amassing material security. The dying man in *Last Things* can think only of material things, and the old man in *A Handful of Soil* wishes to cling to things which are in the last resort impermanent and illusory. The woman in *That Dying Feeling* longs for the permanence, as she sees it, of material things. The young man in *Say No More* thinks that a happy marriage depends only or mainly on owning various luxuries. The king in *Nights and Mornings* gains satisfaction from wielding power over others; so do the businessman in *The Bird, The Forest and the Cage*, the landowner in *A Shady Deal*, Duriodhana in *Draupadi's Prayer*, the concentration camp guards in *Hanging on for Life*, the magician in *In the Bag* and the king in *Standing Up and Sitting Down*.

The pursuit of wealth and power is shown repeatedly in traditional stories to be an inadequate basis of behaviour, and is shown in contrast to values such as love and care, courage and persistence, and mature acceptance of ambiguity and mystery.

❹ Love one another

Maui in *Born from the Waves* feels that he cannot be complete until he is reunited with his family, and family bonds are also central in *The Night We Cried*. Togetherness and companionship are celebrated in *No Lonely Soul*; forgiveness and the absence of bitterness are values in *Recipe for a Happy Marriage*; and there is a passionate desire to save and assist a beloved partner in *Savitri* and in *The Bird, the Forest and the Cage*. The rabbi in *A Double Life* is committed to helping other human beings, so are the monk in *The Way To Go,* Guru Hargobind in *Speaking to the Emperor*, the woman seeking justice in *The Door,* and the people in the cart, the boat and the helicopter in *Means and Ends*. The woman in *That Dying Feeling* desires friendships and companionship, and the story implies that she is right to try to help the person whose cart has overturned even though this involves the ending of her life. *The Monastery* is about, amongst other things, the quality of relationships in an enclosed community. Kevin in *Slender Threads* loves the natural world and acts without bitterness towards the herdsman who beats him.

Sometimes in stories in this book, there are warnings that love and care in a personal relationship require an acceptance of mystery and uncertainty. This, for example, seems to be the teaching of *Return to the Sky* and of *Gifts*, and of the story about mothers and babies, *Hush My Baby*. The first two sisters in *I'm Staying Here* apparently need to go beyond social and political action, and so do the first four teachers in *Five Journeys*. The story entitled *Give and Take* suggests that there is a strong connection between loving and forgiving others and loving and forgiving oneself.

❺ Use your head

Many traditional stories are a celebration of quick-wittedness and intelligence. They thus express and strengthen confidence in human nature and in the capacity of ordinary human beings to find imaginative solutions to their problems. Examples in this book include Shahrazad in *Nights and Mornings*, who tricks the king with her ruse of pretending to go to sleep in the middle of exciting stories; Savitri, who outwits Yama, the god of death and justice, *in Savitri*; Guru Hargobind, who works out a ruse to free all his fellow prisoners in *Speaking to the Emperor*; and the young secretary in *Two Kinds of Idiot*, who outsmarts first the men in the park and then her boss at the office with her sharp and self-confident ingenuity.

Other characters who engage effectively in imaginative thinking to solve a tricky situation include the sufi in *Put to the Test*, the young man's father in *Standing Up and Sitting Down*, the mate in *Out of Fright, Out of Mind*, the Effendi in *A Shady Deal*, the wise woman in *Say No More*, and the birds in *The Bird, the Forest and the Cage*. The young woman in *The Match* tries to use ingenuity, and we admire her for this, but alas she doesn't — apparently — also have sufficient awareness and insight for her ingenuity to be of use to her.

It is striking that trust in human ingenuity often goes hand in hand with a trustful attitude towards the laws, rules and regulations of wider society. Thus, for example, Savitri trusts that Yama will keep his word, and in almost exactly the same way Guru Hargobind trusts the emperor. Similarly the Effendi in *A Shady Deal* trusts the rule of law and the legal system of his society.

Quick-wittedness sometimes involves the creation of art, drama and symbolic actions — as for example in *The Dance of the Star, I'm Staying Here* and *The Needle*. Also it is perhaps not fanciful to suggest that God is using ingenuity and playfulness in *The Football Match*, as is the angel in *Paradise Gardens*.

❻ Love life

Many stories are about delighting in the natural world, or about characters who are unable to take pleasure in the sights, sounds and sensations of everyday life. The old man in *A Handful of Soil* loves the earth of his beloved island, and Maui in *Born From the Waves* develops a great love for nature as an essential part of his growing up. Kevin in *Slender Threads* knows the goodness of his God through the goodness of animals, birds and plants around him. The tree in *A Shady Deal* is perhaps a symbol of the goodness of nature, as is — quite explicitly — the flower in bud held by one of the speakers in *Thrown to the World*. The king in *Nights and Mornings*, in contrast, hates life: but is brought through storytelling to an appreciation of all that life offers.

Human creativity is celebrated in *Look Up, Children* and *The Stonecutter*, and very many stories affirm the essential goodness of life despite the inevitable reality of death: in particular, this is a theme in *A Handful of Soil, In Search of a Cure, Daring to Fly, No Lonely Soul* and *Whoever Comes this Way*. The jokey stories such as *Calm in a Teacup, Is There Anybody There?* and *Say No More* express a sense of fun, and a refusal to give in to depression or despair.

In all oral storytelling, incidentally, there is mutual trust. On the one hand, the listeners trust that the teller will not let them down and that, on the contrary, the story will have a meaningful pattern and a satisfying conclusion. They trust, this is to say, that the story will lead to a new insight and a recognisable truth. But the teller also has to be full of trust — trust that the story will make sense and ring bells, and will bring meaning and pleasure. Insofar as this mutual trust is shown at the end of a story to have been warranted, the story is one of hope. It has, in this sense and to this extent, a happy ending: it is expressive of love of life. The famous story of *Nights and Mornings* is a particularly striking example of the way in which stories can nourish trust and hope, and lead to love of life.

❼ Keep going

Many stories are about a journey to an unknown place. For example, there is the journeying in the Maori myth *Born from the Waves*, and in the Buddhist story of the teachers in *Five Journeys*. The football supporters in *The Football Match* are presumably being urged to forget, or anyway to go beyond, their tribal loyalties. The risk in all such journeying is that there will be a loss of previous identity, orthodoxy and certainty. But stories show, time and again, that this risk has to be taken: life can only be renewed if certain things are allowed to die, even those things which previous generations (including one's own parents) have held to be totally sacred. Courage and dignity are amongst the key values in *The Door, Hanging on for Life,* and *Whoever Comes This Way.*

❽ Look with new eyes

Many of the stories in this book show two or more ways of seeing and understanding the same set of events. Sometimes the message is that the best — or even the only — way to cope with an unchangeable situation is to see it differently, that is, from a different angle, or in a new light. Thus the mother in *In Search of a Cure* sees her own grief differently when she is enabled to know it within a wider context than her own experience alone, and the fearful sailor in *Out of Fright, Out of Mind* is similarly helped to see his situation with a new perspective. The children in *Look Up Children* are encouraged to see the flowers on the hillside differently, and to see also their own growth and gifts in a fresh light. The six blind people in *The Dance of the Star* fail to make connections or see things as a whole, and the couple seeking treasure in *So Near and Yet So Far* have to learn to see familiar surroundings with new eyes. Similarly the main character in *The Stonecutter* comes to see himself differently, and the boss in *Two Kinds of Idiot* is made to see the situation in his office from a different point of view. So are the monks in *The Monastery*, and so is the returning pilgrim in *Gifts*.

❾ Let go

Many stories pose the tension between openness to new experiences on the one hand and acceptance of limits and constraints on the other. And they commend the latter virtue, the humble acceptance of constraints, as being at least as important as the former. Prohibition is a recurring theme: do not open that door, raise the cover of that basket, eat that fruit, ask that question, look in that direction. Stories depend upon curiosity, and indeed celebrate it. Yet also, paradoxically, they are often cautionary tales against certain forms of curiosity, and they commend instead certain qualities of unknowing, humility, patience and agnosticism. Often they embody these virtues in their format as well as their content, by being in some measure ambiguous and mysterious themselves.

The African tale *Return to the Sky* emphasises humility and letting-go in love between two individuals. The traditional Jewish tale-within-a-tale in *Hush My Baby* is about the acceptance of mystery, and so is the jokey story *Calm in a Teacup*. The main teaching of the Indian folktale *I Don't Know What to Do* is about the acceptance of dilemmas in everyday life and about the absence, sometimes, of satisfactory solutions. The shepherd in *The Wandering Sheep* wants her charges to learn from errors and mistakes. The civil servant in *Paradise Gardens* has to learn to accept limits and constraints, and the pilgrim and his wife in *Gifts* have to appreciate that they can't make sense of everything that has happened.

The stories entitled *So Near and Yet So Far*, *The Monastery*, and *The Stonecutter* are all about accepting the situation in which one happens to be. Draupadi puts her trust in Krishna in *Draupadi's Prayer*; the slaves put their trust in their own hopes and strength in *Daring to Fly*; the tortoise trusts posterity and her own dignity in *Whoever Comes this Way*; the old man in *A Handful of Soil* finally has to let go of his love for the island of Crete.

❿ And keep on telling stories

Many of the teachings summarised here stand to an extent in opposition to each other, or else qualify and constrain each other. Accept life, but do not be resigned to fate . . . Keep going, but let go . . . . love one another, but also love yourself . . . look with new eyes, but trust the traditions of the past. It is precisely because the truths expressed in stories are complex and multi-layered that it is in stories that they have to be clothed. A mature philosophy of life is one in which there is a readiness to live with symbolism, metaphor, parable, myth and imagery.

Most of the stories on pages 9-20 recall the importance of metaphor and symbolism, and many refer to the benefits and uses of stories in everyday life. The grandmother in *Thrown to the World* maintains that happiness depends on knowing and sharing stories, and suggests that the subject-matter of many stories is symbolised by the six objects which members of her family hold in their hands: a stone, a bracelet, a prayerbook, a compass, a ring and a flower in bud. The story entitled *Naked Truth* emphasises the importance of symbolism and indirectness. Symbolism is part and parcel of the story-line of *The Dance of the Star*, *The Needle*, and *I'm Staying Here*. Very many of the other stories are presumably to be understood symbolically rather than, or as well as, literally: in particular, perhaps, *Hanging on for Life* and *Daring to Fly*.

Have faith in the past. Don't walk away.
You can't take it with you. Love one another.
Use your head. Love life. Keep going.
Look with new eyes. Let go. And keep on telling
stories. This is humanity. This is the inside of stories.
This is wisdom and hope for changing worlds.

4
From Tadpole to Butterfly

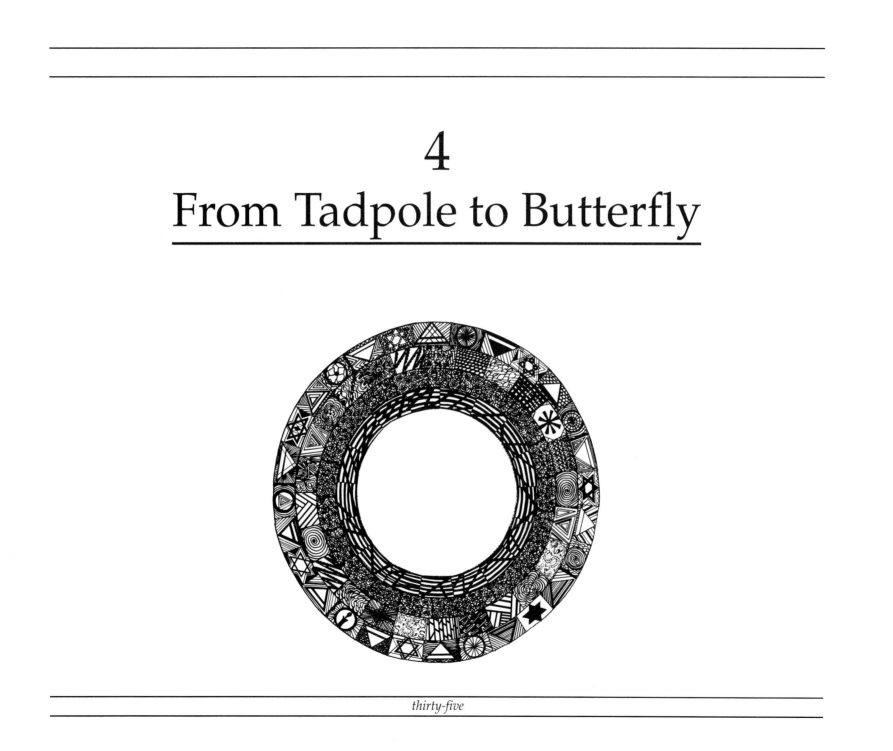

Stages and tasks of living: 50 stories

EMERGING

SEEKING

LOVING

STRUGGLING

Thrown to the World

EMERGING EMERGING EMERGING

It's about this family.

Through cruel ill fortune, the members of this family suddenly found themselves to be refugees from their homeland. They had nowhere to dwell and nowhere to return to: they could only move onwards, outwards, could only be footloose, migrants now for the rest of their lives. The family consisted of an old grandmother, close to the end of her days; her three grown-up children and their partners; and about a dozen grandchildren, including a tiny infant, a few weeks old.

What was to become of them? Where would they find asylum? They debated and deliberated: in the very heart of their trauma they shared their dreams and their hopes concerning the kind of new country they would most like to settle in.

'Basically,' said one of them, fingering a smooth stone, 'everything depends on chance. Obviously we must look after ourselves as well as we can, and we must keep ourselves strong. But at the end of the day what matters is luck, either good luck or bad luck. So let's stop talking and dreaming about this matter. This lifeless stone reminds us that our feelings are irrelevant. All this talk is pointless.'

'Well yes I do agree in many ways,' said a second, stroking a bracelet. 'But we need wealth and riches if at all possible. If I wear this bracelet, and stroke it tenderly every day, there is a good chance, I believe, that we shall become rich and wealthy.'

'That's all very well', said a third, opening a small prayerbook, 'but happiness doesn't just depend on the sun and the scenery. It depends on whether we are are left alone to be ourselves, and to stay exactly as we are. We must be able to continue to speak our own dear language, to tell our children our own special tales and truths, and to be protected in all our ways by our own dear God. This little booklet written in our own language will always remind us: nothing is more important than continuity and stability, and the cherishing and preserving of our past.'

'Yes of course,' said a fourth, taking out a compass, 'that is quite right. But we've got be streetwise, too. This compass I'm holding is a reminder to us that we've got to be sharp and cunning, and trust our own sense of direction. Often we shall have nothing to depend on apart from our own courage and our own quick thinking. These are the qualities we need to be building.'

'That's all very well, ' said a fifth, showing the others a wedding ring. 'It's important that we should be clever and cunning, yes of course, and not afraid to take risks. But it's even more important to love each other. This ring is a symbol of never-ending love. We should let nothing ever get in the way of love. If necessary, it is more important to sacrifice one's own life than to stop loving. That's real bravery, and that's what is perhaps going to be required of us.'

'Of course it is important,' said a sixth, holding up a flower in bud, 'that we should be prepared to love each other. But finally what we are going to need is hope — we need to believe that finally, and deep down, all will be for the best. Look at this bud. It will one day become a beautiful flower. Then one day the flower will change into seeds, and the seeds will fall into the earth, and a new plant will grow. So life will go on, and on and on. There is death, yes, all the time, and terrible misfortune. But also there is always new life.'

The six of them turned to the old grandmother, each of them wanting and expecting her to support their own views. She happened at that moment to be holding the infant, the youngest and the newest of the whole extended family. She stroked the child's face gently, and gazed into the depths of the child's eyes. 'Let us go,' she said, 'to the country where the power and the energy in this child will have the best chance of unfolding into a human being fully alive.' And she added: 'The way to cherish and nourish that power and energy is through telling stories.'

She paused. 'And the stories need to be, you know, about the six small objects which you have all just been showing. 'Once upon a time there was a stone, a bracelet, a prayerbook, a compass, a wedding ring, and a flower in bud.' That's how all stories ought to begin. Drenched in stories such as that, this child will become a human being fully alive.'

The child in her arms smiled. But was the smile grateful and approving, or was it ironic and resigned?

No member of the family could at that stage tell. The future stretched out before them, unknown and featureless, like an untold story.

Born from the Waves

This is the tale of Maui-Potiki, his birth and his boyhood, and his becoming a man. It is the tale too of Taranga his mother, who believed when she first saw him that he could not survive, and of the man Tama-nui-ki-te-Rangi, who loved him as a father.

Taranga his mother did not carry Maui in her womb for nine full months, and on the day he was born he was not ready and alive enough, she was sure, to survive. She took him to the seashore, and kneeling there shivering in the cold wind she cut her hair, and used her hair as a kind of sheet, to swathe her newborn babe. Then with chants and blessings, but neither hoping nor trusting, she threw her darling into the cold waves of the sea.

But the waves were gentle, they were soft and kind. They twined seaweed round the tiny child, and brought him safely floating to another shore. There on the shingle he was found by Tama-mui-ki- te-Rangi. At first, Tama thought that the bundle on the shore was just a heap of rotting seaweed, covered with hungry and swarming flies. It was the crying of the baby, from within the bundle on the deserted windswept shore, that drew Tama close. Tama unwrapped the baby Maui from the weeds and the hair, and took him tenderly to his hearth and home.

Tama taught Maui all he knew. Names, stories, riddles, chants, blessings. How to be cunning, how to use magic, how to be brave. To seek, to dare, to hope, to yearn. To love the wide sky and the hot sun, the fish in the ocean and the birds in the air, the strength and the spread of the towering trees. 'Nature is your mother,' said Tama. 'She will love you and bless you for ever.'

After many years Maui longed to meet his other mother, the woman who had carried him in her womb. He took leave of Tama and both of them wept, for they had done and had woven so much together. But Tama's days on earth were drawing towards an end, and Maui knew that he could never be content if he never saw and touched his mother. He set off.

Maui travelled for many weeks over the earth, through villages and forests, and across mountains and rivers. At long last he came to a lonely village, and felt drawn to a house on the outskirts. He stood close by in hiding. Taranga was there, and she had four sons. All four were strong and tall, and she called to each of them by name. Maui-i-mua, my eldest. . . Maui-i-roto, my second- born. . .Maui-i-taha, my third son. . . Maui-i-pai, my fourth.

Maui-Potiki stepped forward. 'Who are you, stranger?' his mother asked. 'I am Maui-Potiki,' he replied, 'your fifth son.'

'But I have only four sons,' she said. 'Are you sure?' he questioned her, 'are you really sure?'

'Do you come from the north?' she asked, and Maui answered, 'No.'

'Do you come from the south?' she asked, and Maui answered, 'No.'

'Do you come from the west?' she asked, and Maui answered, 'No.'

'Do you come from the east?' she asked, and Maui answered, 'No.'

'Do you come from the waves of the sea?' she asked, and Maui answered, 'Yes, I come from the waves of the sea.'

He told her the story which Tama-nui-ki-te-Rangi had so often through the years told to him. He told how a tiny shivering baby had cried from within a bundle of hair and weed on a deserted windswept shore, and how Tama had taken the babe tenderly to the warmth of his own fireside and home.

Taranga's eyes filled with tears. 'You are my son,' she said. 'I welcome you home.'

Hush My Baby   Jewish

'Is my baby too heavy for her age?' 'Is he underweight?' 'Why doesn't she sleep during the day?' 'Why does he sleep so much?' 'He never stays still for a moment, doctor.' ' She just lies there.'

It seemed to have been a particularly long session at the mother and baby clinic this afternoon. She loved seeing the newborns and the toddlers , but it was a demanding job at the best of times and it had been particularly difficult today: for some reason, there was rather more crying than usual and the noise had been unbearable. So many parents seemed to have one kind of worry after another. She was glad that she had seen all but the very last child and she hoped this one would not be too complicated.

'He's taking all his feeds, is he?' the paediatrician asked.

'Well, yes, I think so... He seems to be eating normally but I wonder if I should put him on cereal. The lady next to me in the hospital, her baby's already on ground rice. Do you think that's a good idea — you hear so many different ideas these days...'

'His weight gain is fine for his age but you could try him on solids if you like — just a couple of spoonfuls at first. But actually mother's milk is still the best — there's no doubt about that — and he certainly looks well on it... ' She tickled the baby under the chin and he gurgled with delight.

'I was wondering, doctor, why his legs are still like that — knock-kneed, I mean.'

'Bring him over to the table, would you, and slip off the bottom of his babygro.'

The infant lay on his back and played with his fingers in the air. 'They do get a little con-stricted before they're born, sometimes, but there's very little to worry about at the moment. Quite often we find that they straighten them-selves out naturally and if they don't there are several things we can do to correct them. There are little shoes that we can give him to wear while he's asleep: you tie them together at the heels and that usually does the trick after a while.' The baby kicked his feet in the air at that point and the doctor and the mother shared a laugh.

'He's absolutely fine... Just do what seems natural — the way our grandmothers did — lots of love and honest-to-goodness common sense. We'll have another look at his legs when he comes in for his next lot of jabs. In the meantime, bring him in if there's anything else bothering you.'

'Well, there's one other thing actually, doctor, but I'm sorry to take up your time. It's this flat bit between his lip and his nose. It seems a bit big, doesn't it? It doesn't run in the family. Why do you think that is?'

The child is perfectly normal, thought the doctor. What could she possibly say to reassure this concerned young mother?

'My grandmother used to say that a baby has a perfect life in the womb; it knows absolutely everything and can see from one end of the world to the other. The dent between its top lip and its nose is caused by an angel who flies down at the very moment it's born and presses a single finger over the baby's lips to hush it. After that the baby spends its whole life learn-ing what it once knew naturally — and without trying.'

In the Dark and the Day

'Come!' he called. 'Come into the house. It's time for supper, and time you were going to bed.'

But the father couldn't persuade his little daughter to come into the house from the garden. She insisted on playing out there until after it was dark. So he made up a story, to frighten her. He told her that there were ghosts in the garden, and that they came out as dusk began to fall, and would harm her if they caught her.

The little girl was terrified. From now on she wouldn't even go out to the garden in the daytime. But her father needed her to help him grow vegetables. So he gave her a lucky charm.

'Wear this round your neck,' he said, 'and you'll be perfectly all right in the daytime. Really, I promise you, the ghosts won't harm you if you wear this charm.'

So she wore the charm round her neck, and everything was all right in the daytime.

I Don't Know What to Do

Announcer: Welcome to another edition of *Childcall*. The lines are open now and our Agony Expert, Pat Payne, is in the studio as usual, waiting to hear from you.

Agony Expert: Hello, everybody.

Announcer: Phone us about anything that's on your mind, anything you'd like help with. Our first caller today must be one of our youngest listeners: she has a problem she needs help with rather quickly. Susan, you're through now.

Agony Expert: Hello, Susan... Hello, can you hear me?... Hello, are you there?

Child Caller: (nervously) Yes.

Agony Expert: Is there something you'd like to share today?

Child Caller: Um, I can't say really...

Agony Expert: Is something wrong at school?

Child Caller: No.

Agony Expert: Is it to do with your friends?

Child Caller: No.

Agony Expert: Do you have a pet you're worried about?

Child Caller: Sort of... but it's about my Mum and Dad, really.

Agony Expert: Oh dear, has anything happened?

Child caller: They're all right now but I'm scared (starts to sob).

Agony Expert: It's all right. Crying does you good.

Child Caller: (sniffs) My Dad's at work but he'll be back soon and my Mum's in the kitchen... My Dad usually does the shopping because he doesn't want my Mum to have much money and he likes to get whatever we have. Yesterday he came home with this really nice steak that he wanted for dinner today.

My Mum took it out this morning to get it ready and then someone came to the door and when she came back Boney was eating it.

Agony Expert: Who's Boney — your brother or sister?

Child Caller: (laughs) No, I haven't got any brothers or sisters. Boney's my dog. Well, really he's a stray but I play with him when I'm lonely and I feed him scraps and he's sort of my dog, I suppose...

Agony Expert: I see... And you're afraid you'll get into trouble when your Mum finds out, are you?

Child Caller: Oh no, my Mum already knows — she saw Boney eating it. That's the trouble — she's got a terrible temper on her, my Mum — and she was that mad with him that she turned the table over on top of him... and she's killed him (breaks down in tears).

Agony Expert: How do you feel about that, Susan?

Child Caller: I feel terrible. And anyway, my Dad will be home soon, you see.

Agony Expert: And then he'll get cross because there's no dinner for him?

Child Caller: Oh no, he's got a dinner... my Mum's cooked Boney!

Agony Expert: I see, your mother has cooked the dog for your father's dinner.

Child Caller: Yes, that's my problem. I don't think she's going to let on and I'm not sure if my Dad will be able to taste the difference — what do you think? If I tell my Dad, he'll kill my mother; but if I don't tell him, he'll eat the dog!

Agony Expert: What you're saying is whatever you do, it's wrong?

Child Caller: Yes.

Announcer: I'm afraid we'll have to leave it there, Susan. We have a lot of other callers on the line. Thank you for phoning in, and the best of luck. Our next listener...

Look Up Children!

'Look up, children! See over there! Those are the flowers. . . So many rich, bright colours. Isn't it beautiful?'

'We want the story again — oh please!'

They gathered round and settled on the grass, some nestling at her feet, others snuggling up against her, two sinking into her lap.

'Well now, a little boy lived here once. He wasn't much older than you but he was very small for his age. The other boys were big enough to track animals with the men and he so wanted to go with them. He used to watch them mount their horses, looking really splendid and grown up; he wished with all his might that he was not so tiny; and he allowed himself to hope that at the very last minute they would stop and turn around and say that he could come with them after all. But they never did.

He gazed with sadness and longing at the distant line of horses and hunters crossing the Plain, until they were no more than specks on the horizon. He knew that they would return that night with glorious tales to tell, and that he would listen with delight as well as envy.

'Don't worry,' his mother always said with a smile. 'You have a special gift. You can carve animals and people from the oddest pieces of wood; you can make useful straps and bags from the tiniest scraps of leather; you can paint pebbles and stones with the brightest berry juices. You are not like the others; you are like yourself. . . and that is what you must strive to be. The others will be remembered in our people's story for their courage in battle and success in the hunt, and we shall sing their praises. But you too will be remembered in our people's story for what you do and are, and we shall sing your praises also.'

He couldn't run like the other boys; he couldn't wrestle; he couldn't shoot with a bow. He wasn't fast enough or big enough or strong enough to do anything important. What did his mother mean? Why should his people sing his praises? How could he be remembered?

He would spend many long hours in the forest and on the hills, collecting wood and stones, and fruits and feathers, for his craft. Gazing into the sky, he wondered what he would become - and how he could ever be a man . . .

One day he saw in the clouds an old man and a young woman, coming towards him. They seemed to be bringing something. The old man laid pots of paints and brushes of the finest hair before him, and said, 'With these you will paint pictures of the warriors' deeds and the visions of the holy ones. When our people see them they will remember them for ever.'

The young woman laid a soft white animal skin before him and said, 'Find a deerskin as soft and white as this. Paint on it the colours of the evening sky.'

Suddenly the clouds parted, the old man and the young woman faded, and a glorious sunset spread before him. He looked at the deerskin and in his mind's eye it glowed with all the vibrant hues of the setting sun. Then the sun disappeared behind the hills and he knew the dream was over. Slowly, he returned to the camp.

Soon he began preparing for the picture. He bound animal hairs together to make brushes; he crushed fruits and leaves and lichen to make paints; he cut wood to make frames; he stretched animal skins to make canvas. He painted with daring and devotion — so that his people would remember — the great hunts of the warriors and the inspiring visions of the wise ones. In his heart he still yearned to ride out with the men and the other boys. But in his heart he treasured also his mother's words and the painting he had pictured.

Every evening he went to the place where he had first seen the image of the sunset, to take it in, to keep it with him. But still he could not paint it on the skins. He yearned to share with his people the vision he had seen, so that they could cherish it for ever. How could he capture the colours? How could he bring it all to life? How could his dream come true?

One night he heard a voice telling him that his time had come, that the next day he would be given what he needed, and that he should take with him the soft white deerskin which he had prepared. He went to the hill again and laid his brushes down while he savoured the last of the sun's rays, drinking in its richness and wonder. In a flash, he saw that his brushes had miraculously been filled with paint. There were shades he had never made, shades he had only ever imagined. Now he had no doubt that he could tell the story of the sunset.

The paint was thick and smooth and he worked with energy and excitement, using one brush after another, until the picture on the skin and the picture in his soul were one — and he was sure at last that his people would have something to remember. Leaving the brushes behind, he hurried back to the camp with the sunset in his hands, and in his heart.

The very next morning, the whole hillside was ablaze with colour, for his brushes had taken root in the ground, and had burst into bloom.

'Look up, children! See over there! Those are the flowers. They blossom every spring on this hill. So many rich, bright colours. Isn't it beautiful?'

The Dance of the Star Hinder

'What is it, my friends, to be a grown-up human being? What is it, my sisters and brothers, to be fully alive?

'Oh my treasures, my comrades, my darlings, I will tell you. My travelling companions on this moonlit planet, here is the message which I am bringing to you.'

She lowered the microphone from her lips, and for a magical moment of stillness there was total silence in the vast stadium. 80,000 fans hung on her words. Not for nothing was she a megastar, one of the most dazzling personalities the world had ever known. All-singing and all-dancing: and now, for a few seconds, all-silent and all-motionless. She raised the mike back to her lips. 'To be fully alive, my friends, is to be like . . . like . . . an ELEPHANT!' And the drummer behind her smashed into action with split-second timing, and chords from the lead guitar smashed into the stadium, and suddenly now, without any warning, she was into her last number of the evening. She sang, she danced.

The climax of the evening was this, her final dance. That final dance said it all.

There were six people in the stadium that night, six out of 80,000, who kept their eyes closed during the megastar's final dance. They were wondering what she meant — 'to be a fully alive human being is to be like an elephant'. They were totally mystified. After the concert was over these six felt that they could never rest unless and until they had found out what the star meant. They went forth, these six fans whose eyes had been closed, to find out.

The first of the fans went to an international airport, and gazed at the jumbo jets ranged there on the tarmac. Such magnificent, human-made beauty and power. To be fully alive, concluded the first fan, is to make things, to bring things into existence, to criss-cross the world with your inventions.

The second fan went to Tuscany in Italy, vaguely assuming from the name that this was a place which had something to do with elephants. Such beautiful buildings, towns and villages, drenched in the wisdom and certainties of past centuries. To be fully alive, concluded the second fan, is to be firmly rooted in tradition and culture.

The third fan went to a zoo, and gazed not only at the elephants but at all the other creatures too. Nature red in tooth and claw, the law of the jungle, the survival of the fittest, unending conflict, pursuit and oppression. To be fully alive, concluded the third fan, is to be involved in politics — in the making of peace and justice, and keeping them in good repair.

The fourth fan went to a gift shop, one which specialised in figures, statues and ornaments made from carved ivory. Such care and love, to create objects which people will give to those whom they love. To be fully alive, concluded the fourth fan, is to to have close friends, and people who love you, and whom you love.

The fifth fan went to a school playground, and listened to the riddles with which the children there were testing each other. (How can you tell if there's an elephant in your fridge? — You can't close the door. What do you say to a mad elephant who's just about to set a pack of crazed bull pit terriers on you? — 'Sir'.) Such a sense of absurdity, of life as basically ridiculous. To be fully alive, concluded the fifth fan, is to have a sense of humour and fun.

The sixth fan called in at a back-street shop selling second-hand records, and listened to an old song: 'Nellie the Elephant packed her trunk, and said good-bye to the circus'. Such sublime lack of interest in daily work, such wonderful neglect of chores and duties. To be fully alive, concluded the sixth fan, is to be detached from the demands of your everyday life.

After a while, these six fans met up with each other. They argued, argued, argued, argued. Making things. . . being rooted in tradition . . . making and maintaining peace and justice . . . loving and being loved . . . having a sense of humour and fun . . . being detached: they had these six separate points of view about what the star had said, and they argued and argued.

The more they argued, the less they felt themselves to be alive.

'Pity you didn't watch the star's final dance that evening,' said someone to them. 'If only your eyes hadn't been shut.'

'What do you mean?' they asked. 'What do you mean?'

But they were not alive enough to hear the answer.

The Wandering Sheep

A sheep found a hole in the hedge, and scrambled through. He wandered far over the countryside, and got very, very lost.

There were wild rottweiler dogs around and they attacked and chased after the sheep. The sheep ran and ran, was utterly petrified.

The shepherd went out looking for the sheep, and found it. She fought off the dogs, and carried the sheep lovingly back to the fold.

'You must repair the hedge,' people said to the shepherd.

'No,' she said. 'I cannot fence them in. I love my sheep too much.'

So Near and Yet So Far   Jewish

Rebecca sat bolt upright in bed and dug her husband in the ribs. 'I've had that dream again... Wake up! It was really clear tonight as well.' And she described the vision that she had seen: precious jewels and piles of money were locked in a heavy wooden casket, buried two metres deep; on the ground, or maybe above it, was a solid iron slab. And there was running water, too.

'Three nights in a row is really something, Becky,' was Joe's initial comment. 'Who'd have thought?'

'But this time it was different, Joe. You see — now don't laugh, please — this time I heard someone telling us if we could lift the iron slab it would all be ours.'

'What someone?' enquired Joe.

'I don't know — just someone.'

In the days that followed, Joe asked around about where the place could be. Without doubt, the treasure must be buried underneath the black iron bridge over the river in the mother city. Yes, that made absolute sense. It had to be...

The journey was long and hard. For stretches along the way, people gave Becky and Joe a lift but the rest of the time they walked — in rain or shine, up hill and down dale, through towns and forests, until finally they reached the magical place of Rebecca's dreams.

When they came to the bridge it was definitely black iron, but it was guarded day and night. They did not dare search for the treasure but wandered nervously over the bridge waiting for the dark to hide them.

One morning, the captain of the guards approached Rebecca. 'I cannot help noticing that you are very interested in the bridge,' he said, 'and in what lies below.' It was then that she told him about her dream — the place, the voice, the journey.

'You've come a long way for a dream,' scoffed the captain. 'I have a vision, too. It is of a poor couple — Joseph and Rebecca. They have precious jewels and piles of money locked in a heavy wooden casket, buried two metres deep; on the ground, or maybe above it, is a solid iron slab. And there is silent running water, too'.

The search under the bridge seemed pointless and Rebecca and Joe hurried back. The journey was long and hard. For stretches along the way, people gave Becky and Joe a lift but the rest of the time they walked — in rain or shine, up hill and down dale, through towns and forests, until they finally reached home.

There was their black iron stove beside the well, just as it had always been. Surely not? They dug and dug until they hit a wooden casket. It was filled with precious jewels and piles of money. But in it there was also something Rebecca had never dreamed — a tiny scroll which read 'So near and yet so far'.

Five Journeys   Buddhist

An urgent call came to the great Lama of the north from the Lama of the south, asking for a wise and holy teacher to be sent to instruct young people in the south about the purpose of living. To everyone's astonishment the great Lama sent five teachers instead of one. Mysteriously he explained : 'We shall be fortunate if one of them gets to the Lama of the south.'

The group of five set off. They had been on the road for several days when a messenger came running up to them and cried : 'There is a terrible famine in our village, the rains and the crops have failed, both beasts and people are starving, many have already died. Stay with us, we beg you, care for us, teach us knowledge of science and of nature.' — 'I would not be a Buddhist,' said one of the five teachers sent by the Lama of the north, 'if I did not stop here, and provide knowledge and assistance for these suffering people.' The other four continued.

A few days later the four came to a city where some of the people on the streets exclaimed urgently to them : 'The governors of this city are uncaring and cruel. Stay with us here, we beg you, and help us to resist and to replace the people in power here, and to govern ourselves in justice and in peace.' — 'I would not be a Buddhist,' said one of the teachers sent by the Lama of the north, 'if I did not stop here, and join in resistance, politics and government.' The other three continued.

Some days later the three came to a town where there were frantic quarrels and arguments amongst members of different religious groups. 'Help us, we beg you,' said some of the people, 'to understand and to tolerate each other's festivals and customs. So that each person here feels rooted in their own tradition and history, but also feels respect for the traditions and stories of others.' — 'I would not be a Buddhist,' said one of the teachers sent by the Lama of the north, 'if I did not stop here, and help the people to calm down, and to live with each other in harmony and peace.' The other two continued.

A few days later the two came to a small settlement where all the people seemed marvellously happy. There were dances and games, paintings and music, embraces and laughter. There was ripening fruit on the trees, there were solid houses and homes, everyone had challenging and valuable work. 'Settle with us here, we beg you,' said the people, 'set up home here, enjoy sexual love, nurture and cherish new human beings, join us here in building the future.' — 'I would not be a Buddhist,' said one of the teachers sent by the Lama of the north, 'if I did not stop and make my dwelling here, and enjoy the pleasures of everyday life.' The other continued.

Eventually the fifth teacher reached the Lama of the south, and began there the work which had been requested, and which was required, that of instructing the young people about the purpose of living.

The Monastery

The monastery was not a happy place. The monks were envious of each other, they often complained behind each other's backs, they often lost their tempers with each other, and cursed and swore at each other. Sometimes they even came to blows.

There was no joy in the monastery, and no valuable work ever got done. The monks were hopeless at praying.

One day the widow of a rabbi came to live in a ruined hovel near to the monastery's gates. One of the young monks went to visit her.

'You can't come into our monastery, you know,' said the young monk. 'It's for Christians only, we don't allow Jews.'

' Yes, I know,' said the old woman, 'I am quite content to live in this ruined hovel.'

'But why have you come to this region?' asked the young monk, 'There's nothing here for you.'

' I have come to this region,' replied the widow of the rabbi, 'because my husband told me before he died that I would find that the Messiah is resident here, living in disguise.'

'The Messiah is living in disguise in this region ?' asked the young monk, amazed.

'Yes, I believe so,' replied the old woman.

'I suppose what you mean is that Christ has come again,' said the young monk. 'He must be in our monastery,' he added, and he hastened back into the monastery to tell the others.

One of us, the word quickly got round, is Christ in disguise. But who, who ? They didn't know which of the monks it could be, so they began treating everyone, absolutely everyone, in the monastery as if he was the Christ. Their quarrels ceased, there was no more envy, no more anger and cursing, no more criticisms and complaints. The monastery became a very peaceful place, a place full of joy, and of work, and of prayer.

The young monk forgot all about the old widow in the hovel, and the other monks didn't even know that she was there. One day many years later, however, the young monk went again to the ruined hovel near the monastery gates where he had first met her. She was still there. He remembered what she had told him. 'You said that your husband told you before he died that if you came to this region you would find that the Christ is resident here,' he recalled, 'and that he would be living here in disguise.'

'That's right,' said the old woman, 'my husband said that the Messiah would be here.'

'But I don't understand,' said the young monk. 'Where is he? Where exactly in this region is the Messiah living ?'

Give and Take Jewish

The door of her workshop opened and her husband looked in. 'I'm home, love!' He came across to kiss her. 'Leave that now,' he said. 'You've done enough and you know it'll still be there after Yom Kippur.' He always said that — it'll still be there — and he always finished work early before the Sabbath or a festival. He never let anything get in the way of something really important, and he liked to be ready in good time.

'Won't be a moment,' she replied. 'Go on up and have your bath, dear.' The children would be in from school any minute. It was hard being a wife and a mother and having a business to run, and she felt that she never did anything properly. Still, they never complained, bless them. She heard her husband moving about in the kitchen above. She was lucky to have him, she thought, such a good man. He does more than his share around the house. She switched off her sewing machine, rolled up the cloth, and carefully put her scissors away.

It had been a rushed day. She spent the morning cooking for supper, to begin the day-long fast, and also for the breaking of the fast the following evening. A friend of hers had had a lot of worries lately and she felt bad that she hadn't been to see her, so she phoned and they both felt better. She also popped round to her parents' at midday: she wanted to say to them that she was sorry, but didn't know exactly what she was sorry for. The look in their eyes told her, though, that whatever it was they understood... and they loved her anyway. When she got home, she went back to her dressmaking table. She never liked unfinished work, and she hoped against hope that she would just have time to put the final touches to the garment she had promised.

The children came back from school and her husband bustled about getting them washed and changed, and organising them to lay the table. She had a good soak and put on a clean dress. Then they all sat down to a meal, ending with a drink of water — seven sips was the custom in their household. When the table was cleared she lit the candles and said the blessing for the Day of Atonement.

It is a good day, she thought, a blessed chance to be especially close to God, a chance to confess, a chance to be forgiven. Everything would be all right now, she felt. She had made her peace with her husband and children, and they had made their peace with her. She had done all that was humanly possible. Besides, she knew that other people always forgave her more easily than she forgave herself.

The atmosphere in the synagogue that evening was electric. There was always a certain awe on Yom Kippur, a precious feeling that God would be kind, and that atonement would flow from sincere confession and intense prayer.

'For the sins we have committed . . .' the congregation sang with honesty and devotion, and then fell silent. She reflected on her life, and threw herself on the mercy of God. She was weeping as she recalled the year that had gone and did not know she was speaking out loud.

What a miserable creature I am. . .

There are so many good causes that I ought to support, and don't...

I could have been a better friend. . .

My own children are practically in rags. . .

I know I take my dear husband for granted. . .

My donations to charity have slipped. . .

The community needs all of us to pull our weight. . .

I haven't bothered to keep up my Jewish studies. . .

My wonderful parents deserve more of me at their age. . .

I always seem to be behind with the orders. . .

My heart isn't in the right place. . .

My mind keeps wandering, wandering. . .

Dear God, please forgive me, you who are so. . .

'Come to think of it, God,' she continued, 'you haven't had such a good year yourself! The world is far from perfect, and a lot of it is down to you. There was that dreadful earthquake in Central America... those awful floods in Bangladesh... that terrible train crash in France... the thousands of homeless people sleeping out every night in our own cities... that dear old lady battered to death in her own flat — and just for her pension book... those poor children in that boarding school with that dreadful headmaster — ugh! I shudder to think of it! ...Think of all the happiness you could have created, and didn't. Think of all the suffering you could have ended, and didn't. You have taken mothers from their children and children from their mothers... It seems to me that you need forgiveness as much as I do! But I'm a reasonable woman and I'll make you an offer you can't refuse. I'll forgive you if you'll forgive me. Is that a deal?'

The woman in the seat behind her had heard every word. 'Whatever are you saying?' she asked. 'Don't you know who you're talking to? You had God really squirming in the palm of your hand. Why did you let God off so lightly?'

No Lonely Soul

It is always at night that the Banshee comes. As lights go on all over the sky and factory sirens blast, she drifts across the sky. As birds fly home to their nests and cats come out to prowl, she gazes down. As supermarkets close and workers say goodnight, she wends her way. As cinema queues grow long and pubs fill up with regulars, she hovers overhead.

When there's no room in the night for day, the Banshee waits her chance.

Milk-fed babies are tucked in cots and wished sweet dreams; bath-scrubbed children are read a story and then bundled into bed. It is always at night that the Banshee comes, seeking a lonely soul. Mothers and fathers sigh and sink into a chair. They speak of the day just gone, the day to come, the night between. She sees them sitting close. Finding no lonely soul, the Banshee turns away.

Arm in arm, two lovers stroll along, watching each other's words breathed in the cold, crisp air. They pause in doorways and share a kiss. Finding no lonely soul, the Banshee turns away.

It is always at night that the Banshee comes, singing her mournful song. 'Here, boy!' a teenager calls to his dog, and his faithful friend comes running. Finding no lonely soul, the Banshee turns away.

Her wispy tune wafts down the corridor of the labour ward and a woman screams in pain. Her partner mops her brow and strokes her hand. 'I'm with you, darling. I know it's bad.' Finding no lonely soul, the Banshee turns away.

It is always at night that the Banshee comes, binding her hair in the trees. The farmer hears the chickens clucking and flapping their wings in terror. 'Foxes!' she cries, and rushes out to make safe the coop. Finding no lonely soul, the Banshee turns away.

Her eerie music haunts the children's room. 'Daddy, Daddy! I've had a nasty dream!' a little one cries out and the father hurries down the hall. He holds her tight and drives away her fear. Finding no lonely soul, the Banshee turns away.

It is always at night that the Banshee comes, luring lost creatures with flame. Gasping for breath in the billowing smoke, an old man crouches in fright. 'It's all right,' a friendly neighbour says. 'The fire's down there. Come on out our side.' Finding no lonely soul, the Banshee turns away.

The Banshee's chill wind creeps into the shabby hostel room. A little girl pulls a blanket over her sleeping brother's shoulders. Finding no lonely soul, the Banshee turns away.

As party-goers stagger home and milk-carts rattle, the Banshee hovers overhead. As markets open up and machines whirr into action, she wends her way. As morning tea is poured and sleepy eyes are rubbed 'Good morning!', she gazes down. As letters drop through boxes and reluctant children dress for school, she drifts across the sky.

When there's no room in the day for night, the Banshee bides her time. It is always at night that the Banshee comes.

The Night We Cried Jewish

The snow fell heavily that day as every day that winter in the camp. It was so thick you couldn't see your hand in front of your face and the blizzard was so strong you could hardly stand, let alone walk. The job of clearing snow — another vicious joke the guards were playing — was pointless and impossible. 'We can't do it!' some of the girls protested. 'Can't you see we're falling over? It'll kill us!' A bitter laugh was the guards' reply. 'And what do you think you're here for?' They'd made their point — they could dangle death — and now they didn't need us shovelling snow: they took us to the factory and made us work. A whole day and night we worked — no food, no water, no rest, nothing.

I felt like an old woman, though I was just a girl at the time. I had long since stopped wondering why the other girls seemed so frail and worn — their faces gaunt and lined — for I must have seemed the same to them. And when I gazed into their eyes, I saw looking back at me the agony and anguish that I shared. Even the cruelty of the guards no longer really shocked: it was their way, and it had become our way, too. I had suffered too much — and seen so many others suffering too — there was almost nothing left to feel. My fingers, and my heart, were numb.

And yet I knew a little warmth, the glow of having my mother near, the hope we both cherished of seeing once again my father and my brother.

She was waiting in the barracks that night and had saved her soup. 'Here,' she said, drawing the bowl from under her blanket. 'It's still warm. It'll make you warm.'

Her body was broken. She needed the soup. I needed her to live. 'I cannot take it, Mother, it's your soup.'

'But you have eaten nothing for a day. I would rather spill it than take it.' Her body was broken but her spirit unbeaten.

'Mother, please, you must. . .'

But I could tell my pleadings were in vain. There was no way out: we both wanted the other to survive, to be nourished, to feel warm. We wanted this more than anything else in the world, more than anything either of us wanted for herself. I looked at her; she looked at me; and for a moment we were paralysed, locked into our love for each other, and both unable to take a single sip of the soup. Then slowly, deliberately, my mother tipped the bowl over. The thin but precious liquid trickled onto the ground. Our tears fell more freely than I have ever known. We hugged more tightly than I have ever felt. And then the morning came.

* * * * * * * * * *

My brother had survived the war, but had been wounded in the head. His childhood, too, was lost for ever.

And then one day we met a man who'd been with my father in the camps — and saw him die. He told us what had happened: how fatigue had overcome him, how he could walk no further, and how they had shot him . . . He told us when it was: the night my mother spilt the soup, the night we cried.

Savitri Hindu

'Why is your heart so heavy, Savitri, why are you not eating? For three days now you have been simply sitting in silence and prayer before this holy fire. Why, Savitri, why? Please tell me, please let me help you.'

Savitri shook her head sadly. How could she possibly tell her dear husband the truth? How could she bring herself to reveal to him the prayers and the pleadings which she had been making in the silence of her heart over these last three terrible days?

Today was the day of their first wedding anniversary, and should have been a day of rejoicing. But Savitri was sorrowful because she knew that on this day her husband Satyvan was doomed to die. She had been warned in a prophecy, a few days before the marriage, that he would die exactly one year after the wedding.

For the last three days she had refused to eat, and had been praying before the sacred fire at their home. She felt now that her struggle had been in vain. A demon had thrown a curse on her husband's whole family — his father was blind and his mother was crippled, and both were penniless. Once, in the past, they had been king and queen of a prosperous and happy country. And Satyvan himself was doomed to die on his first wedding anniversary. Savitri had done her best to empty her mind of all worry and thought, and to sit wholly still and calm, hoping desperately that her inner purity and stillness would enable her husband's life to be saved. She feared that she had not done enough, though, and that his death was now certain.

They lived in a poor house in the middle of a forest. 'I am going,' said Satyvan, 'into the depths of the forest to cut wood for the sacred fire.' He picked up an axe. 'Let me come with you!' said Savitri immediately. 'I must come with you.'

'No. You are too weak. You haven't eaten for three days. You cannot possibly come with me into the inner depths of the forest.'

'Of course I can come, and I must, and I will.' He did not argue further, and the two set out together, though Savitri was indeed very weak from her fasting.

They were walking through a small clearing when Satyvan suddenly dropped his axe, stumbled and fell. He lay still on the ground. All the birds in the forest fell silent — parrots, mynah birds, magpies, jays. A family of monkeys stopped its chattering and looked down from their tree. The whole forest was deathly still.

Yama, the god of death, emerged from the deepest forest. He was dressed all in dark rusty red, and in his hand he carried a grey cord, tied in a noose. He came to where Satyvan lay, and using his noose he pulled Satyvan's soul slowly and carefully from his body. He turned, and began to go back into the deepest part of the forest.

Savitri followed him. 'I beg you, I beg you,' she said, 'return my husband to life. I wanted so much to save him.'

'No,' said Yama, 'go back to his body, and ensure he has a dignified funeral.'

'I cannot,' said Savitri, 'I beg you to have mercy. Surely you are a god of mercy as well as of justice.' Yama was touched by her devotion. 'I will grant you one favour,' he said. 'Ask anything at all, except that your husband should be restored to life.'

'Very well,' she said. 'Please grant that my husband's parents may be healthy again, and full of strength and energy.'

'It is done,' said Yama. 'When you return, you will find them restored to good health. Now, go back to your husband's body.'

'I cannot. I wish to go with him into death.'

Yama was again touched by her devotion. 'I will grant you a second favour,' he said. 'Ask anything at all, except that your husband should be restored to life.'

'Please,' she said, 'may my husband's parents be restored to their previous position as king and queen.'

'It is done,' said Yama. 'When you return, you will find them ruling their country. Now go back to your husband's body. After a period of mourning you will find that time will heal your sadness, and you will one day have another husband.'

'Never!' exclaimed Savitri. 'You surely know perfectly well that I shall remain single now for the rest of my life.'

Again Yama was touched by her devotion. 'I appreciate,' he said, 'that I cannot really expect you ever to marry again. You fasted for three days, and I will grant you a third favour. But this is the last. Ask anything at all, except that your husband should be restored to life.'

'Please,' she said, 'may my father and mother have many, many grandchildren.' — 'Of course,' said Yama. 'They shall have thousands of descendants, like stars in the sky.'

Now Savitri was clever as well as persistent and loving. She pointed out that her parents had only one child, herself, and that if they were to have grandchildren her husband would have to be restored to life. Yama knew that he was defeated. He was a god of justice, and had to keep his word. He returned the soul to Satyvan's body, and departed. Satyvan woke up.

'What happened?' he asked. 'You have been asleep,' whispered Savitri, stroking his face. She began to sing to him. 'Why is your heart so light?' he asked. She did not say.

She sang from that day onwards every day for the rest of her life. 'Why are you always praising?' people would ask. 'Why is your heart so light?' She said nothing, and nobody knew. The birds of the forest knew, though — parrots, mynah birds, magpies, jays. So did a family of monkeys.

Return to the Sky

Once there was a young chief. He had many very fine black and white cattle. He kept them in a beautiful green pasture near to his village.

Every morning he would go out to the green pasture, and his cows would give him wonderful pure milk, warm, frothing, wonderful in its goodness and strength.

One morning, to his great surprise, the cows had no milk — there was no milk for him. The same thing happened the next morning. And again the next, and the next. He resolved that he would hide in a thicket close to the pasture, and watch what happened.

This he did. In the middle of the night the sky above him opened, and a rope came snaking down to the ground. Then climbing down the rope came many beautiful young women. Each carried a calabash, and each filled her calabash with milk from his cows, pure and very white, and full of goodness and strength. He watched in amazement. When they had filled their calabashes with milk, the young women went back to the rope and returned to the sky, and they let no drop of milk fall.

One young woman was slightly slower than the others. The young chief sprang forward, and ran across the green pasture.

He caught hold of the woman. 'Please, please, stay with me,' he pleaded, 'be my wife, live with me for ever.'

'I will come down from heaven and live with you,' replied the young woman, 'on two conditions.'

'Yes,' said the young chief, 'what are the two conditions?'

'First, that I may bring with me a very special woven basket which I have.'

'Yes, of course, and what is the second condition?'

'The second condition is that you will not lift the lid of the basket, and look inside, until I tell you that you may.'

'Very well,' said the young chief. The young woman lived with him as his wife for many years. Her beautiful woven basket stood at the door of their hut, and they passed it every time they went in or out. The young chief never lifted its cover.

One day his wife was away from the village in the fields, and the young chief was feeling that day very lonely and depressed, very unsure of himself. He noticed the beautiful woven basket at the door of the hut. Why shouldn't I lift the cover and look inside, he wondered.

He knelt down and lifted the cover of the basket. He looked inside. The basket was empty. He replaced the cover.

Towards the end of the day, his wife returned. She had been tending the cattle in the green pasture. 'What have you done today ?' she asked.

'Nothing,' he replied, 'except...'

'Yes ?'

'I opened your beautiful woven basket and looked inside.'

Her eyes filled with tears. 'And what did you see ?'

'Nothing,' he replied, 'nothing. The basket was empty.'

The young woman knelt down and lifted the cover from the basket, and looked inside. Her eyes were brimming with tears. 'No,' she said,' the basket was not, and it is not, empty. I keep the treasures of the sky in here — the stars which sparkle, the sun which rises and warms and dances, and the moon which in the dark is an ever returning promise of light. One day, if you had waited, you would have seen them. But now I must go, I must return to my home in the sky.'

And she left him, taking her basket with her. He wept. He wept with sadness that he had lost her, and that he would never see her again. He wept also with gladness — gladness that he had known her. And gladness that another time would surely come when he might see the treasures of the sky — the stars which sparkle, the sun which rises and warms and dances, and the moon, which in the dark is an ever returning promise of light.

Recipe for a Happy Marriage

BULLY-BOY HUSBAND TAKES THE CAKE

A violent husband who beat his wife yesterday may get away with it, according to a police spokesperson.

WORRIED neighbours burst into the strife-torn Cochin home of Preeti Mahadeva, 21, and her power-crazed husband Manu, 24, when they heard her heart-rending cries for help.

The President announced last week a government enquiry into the rising tide of domestic violence and marital break-up in modern society.

Asked why she refused to give him 'thitthey', Preeti, relaxed and out of danger, explained, 'I didn't know what he was talking about! I've never even heard of it! He claimed my mother had just given him some but she couldn't possibly! That's when he started having a go at me.'

Breaking down

BREAKING down, she was comforted by her sister Lakshmi, a typist with the Water Board. Then she continued, 'My arms and legs were swollen and started coming up in funny lumps. 'Stop it! ' I pleaded, 'You're giving me 'kozhukkatta'!'

I forgive him, says battered wife.

Kozhukkatta are typical Malayali rice cakes, flavoured with sugar and coconut and formed into balls. By strange coincidence, her mother had served them when her son-in-law had visited her earlier in the day.

Shrimati Rukka Monipally, whose family had lived in the street for generations, was the first to hear the young wife's screams and raised the alarm. She found the victim cowering in a corner and sobbing like a baby. She was bruised all over her slender body and her arms and legs were covered in large lumps, the concerned widow told reporters yesterday evening.

Wild animal

DESPERATE relatives pinned Manu, a graduate engineer specialising in hydrodynamics, to the wall of the family courtyard and are believed to have prevented further outbursts.

'I've never seen anything like it,' said a friend who asked not to be named. 'He was like a wild animal. Not like him at all.'

Recovering in her parents' home in Alleppey and wringing a handkerchief as she spoke, Preeti gave *The Recorder* an exclusive interview late last night. 'I knew something was wrong as soon as he came home. He demanded some 'thitthey' like my mother had given him.'

Asked why she refused this reasonable request, Preeti, relaxed and out of danger, explained, 'I didn't have a clue what he was talking about.'

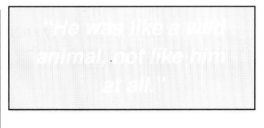

Cup of tea

MEANWHILE Manu Mahadeva was in a subdued mood. 'I don't know what came over me,' he said over a cup of tea. 'I came home from Preeti's mother's all full of excitment. I must ask Preeti to make them for me sometime, I thought. I kept saying the name to myself over and over again: 'ko-zhuk-kat-ta', 'ko-zhuk-kat-ta' when I sud-

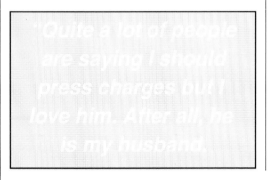

denly lost my balance and fell off my bike into the canal. 'Thitthey' I called out in discomfort and annoyance — and the name of the cakes went right out of my head!'

While Preeti's mother and sisters prepared the evening meal, she began to look ahead.

Father and uncle

'I'LL definitely make him kozhukkattas when I've got the use of my hands back. My father and my uncles always adored them. It was their mother that gave my mother the recipe when she got married. Nobody makes them much any more and I didn't know Manu liked them. There's a lot I don't know about him really, I can see that now. Quite a lot of people are saying I should press charges but I love him. After all, he is my husband.'

Secret ingredients??

QUESTIONED about any secret ingredients in the traditional rice cakes, Preeti's mother said, 'No comment.'

The Match Jewish

The staff at the dating agency were very understanding and helpful, and she was glad that she had finally plucked up courage to go there. Still, she was a bit nervous about the whole thing, and very frightened that it would all end up with her being rejected yet again.

'The trouble is, I never know what to say to a man,' she told the matchmaker when they had chosen someone for her to meet. 'And what if he's as shy as I am?'

'No problem at all, my dear. There are certain subjects that everybody is interested in. It's just a matter of getting started. Just remember the 3 Fs Rule — food, family and philosophy. Those are the three things to talk about.'

He had a friendly, open face and she hoped he would be gentle.

'Do you like ice-cream?' she ventured, trying out the first 'F', food.

'No, not really,' he replied, and was silent.

That's a pity. But never mind. She still had two to go.

'Do you have a sister?'

'No.'

Oh dear, that's both food and family gone. Only one left. What was it? Oh yes, philosophy.

'If you did have a sister, do you think she would like ice-cream?'

Gifts muslim

He had so much to tell. So much had happened on the way. The donkey driver and his hilarious stories . . . that delicious coffee served in all the old Ottoman towns they had passed through . . . the smell of leather tanning . . . the exquisite carpets hung up for sale . . . the sound of beating copper. And then of course all the events and experiences of the holy city of Makka: the perfection of the Ka'aba . . . the excitement of the swirling crowds . . . the freshness of the water at ZamZam. . . and the awesome hush of the desert camp at night.

There was almost too much to tell. And his darling Aisha — what had happened to her? Four long years and there had been no word between them. He couldn't wait to see her lovely face again, to hold her in his arms. And little Muhammad was just a baby when he left. He wouldn't remember his father, of course, but Aisha would have told the little one all about his father, and made him proud. He would surely come running, when he saw him, and jump up on his shoulders, full of joy.

The street was as it had been — nothing changed — yet out of every window came a shout, 'Welcome! Allah be praised!' And there she was, his bride, standing in the doorway like a queen — and little Muhammad clinging to her dress. She looked at him. He looked at her. If only eyes could speak...

From his bag he brought exquisite gifts of inlaid wood and tapestry, rare perfumes and prayer beads, sugared dates and roasted nuts. And on the top — most wondrous of all — he gently laid a precious copy of the Holy Qur'an, illuminated pages of those sacred words on hand-rolled parchment, bound in leather, clasped with gilt.

Little Muhammad snuggled up and he ruffled the small boy's hair. He fed him dates and almonds, and told him of the camels and the sand... And then another child toddled up, a little girl with curly hair and eyes like stars. 'And who are you, sweet one?'

'That's Fatima,' Aisha said. 'She's just turned three. You remember, dear, the night before you left...?'

He smiled, then drew his tiny daughter to his chest. 'Let's see what Daddy has for you — oh yes, some shiny beads, a wooden horse.'

'Can Khadija have one, too?' and she ran to show her baby sister what he'd brought.

Fear gripped him now. 'Aisha, who is this?'

'This isn't easy, not for you or me. We are only human, you and I. We never know what life will bring. Please listen. I will explain. Try to understand. You see...'

Through the open window came a baby's cry. She ran inside.

Slender Threads

I shall always remember the moment I first met Kevin face to face. I hadn't ever been in love before and couldn't have put that name to my feelings then. But I certainly felt something very special for him, and part of me secretly hoped that he might feel something special for me, too.

I had seen him before, of course, but always from a distance. He didn't seem at all like the other men I knew, the farmers and herdsmen who lived in our valley. They laughed and shouted a lot; they always seemed to be busy doing things; they were often in a hurry. And I have to say that some of them could be quite rough at times. Kevin had an air of peace about him; he moved slowly and silently, as if he had all the time in the world; and as he walked he would gaze at the trees and flowers that grew beside the path and the birds that flew above. Why did he live here, all alone, I wondered, what did he have, what did he know, what had put him so deeply in touch with everything around him, what was he that was so very different?

That day in particular I felt strongly drawn to him. I can't explain it but it was almost as if I heard a voice inside me telling me to seek him out . . . and come to know him. I slipped away from the others and made my way up the hill towards the upper lake. The grass was soft under my feet and the sun was warm on my back. The fragrance of the flowers and the songs of the birds seemed sweeter than ever. And it was, without doubt, the holiest and most beautiful day of my life. I couldn't possibly have known where he might be but I was somehow carried there by a force from beyond me and a presence within me.

And then I found him . . . He was sitting in his hut, reading from a book, with his arms resting on the window ledge and his hands stretched out to the sky. I half hoped he would turn and see me; I half hoped that he wouldn't, that I could simply stand there for ever and stare at him. I don't know how long I stayed like that — perhaps a moment, perhaps a lifetime. Then suddenly a blackbird flew down, landed in Kevin's open upturned palm, and began building a nest in it, with twigs and leaves. At first, Kevin seemed unconscious of it but after a while he tilted his head to look at his hand . . . and he smiled. Oh, what a smile! I shall never forget it! It was more than my poor heart could bear and I backed away. I returned the way I had come and joined the others in the pasture.

It was milking time by then, and the herdsmen were bringing the cows in.

I stole away to Kevin's hut every day after that, and every day I ventured a little closer. The bird kept returning, too, and later laid her eggs in the nest in Kevin's hand. Still he had not moved. Still he was reading from his book. Still his arms were reaching up to heaven. What kind of a man is this, I desperately wanted to know, and what did he think of me? Was he even aware that I existed? He must have realised that I was there, but he had never shown it.

I knew my life would change, and I began to feel quite different — fuller, richer, more loving, more myself. And I wasn't the only one who noticed. The herdsmen looked at me with new eyes and asked each other where I went in the daytime, and what could possibly have happened to me.

In time, the eggs in the nest in Kevin's hand hatched, and the little birds flew away. Kevin lowered his arms and closed his book. I sidled towards him and he held me in his gaze. All the love in the world welled up in me, my whole body tingled and my shyness fell away. He smiled that smile again and this time it was for me . . . He was inviting me to him and I stepped boldly forward. I rubbed against his side, whimpering and gasping with delight, and he put his arm around me. There was tenderness and purity in our touch and I knew at once that I had come close to God. This gentle, holy man who had given himself in suffering for a tiny bird, who was loving life and living love, had cast his light on me. I was both humbled and uplifted.

I nuzzled against him as he led me to the lakeside, all the while fondling my neck. We drank from the cool, clear water and then settled on the grass. He cradled my head, stroked my nose, kissed my brow, and whispered a prayer in my ear. It was perfection.

The shouts of the herdsmen interrupted our bliss and called me back to the cowshed, but I knew the oneness I had found with Kevin would never leave me. That night my milk flowed freely and abundantly. 'I expect she's found new pastures,' one of the herdsmen said. 'This could be good for us all.'

He must have followed me the next day. When he found me, I was licking Kevin's rough clothes as he said his daily devotions. On seeing this, the herdsman flew into a rage, though I couldn't understand why. He started yelling at Kevin, cursing and damning him; and then he kicked him and beat him furiously with his stick. But Kevin never opened his mouth.

Tears rolled down my cheeks. The man who had given me so much, who cared for all creatures and who saw in creation the power and love of the creator, stood with his head bent low, despised and rejected. I wanted to end his affliction. I wanted to heal his wounds. But I had no words.

The herdsman drove me back, all the while thrashing my belly. That night our milk was poor and thin. The calves became frenzied and foamed at the mouth, and the cows ran wild and butted them with their heads. The herdsman was afraid he would lose all his cattle. But he could not end our affliction. He could not heal our wounds.

In the morning he returned to Kevin, and I followed him. He fell on his knees. 'I have done you wrong. Please forgive me,' the herdsman said. 'I was frightened when I saw you. You seemed so strange and yet so special. It made me feel bad inside. I don't know who you are or why you are living here like this. I don't understand why you didn't hit me back or even speak out when I insulted you.'

And then Kevin spoke.

'I am a servant of the Lord. I have chosen the way of the hermit, in harmony with the earth, the water and the sky; alone with the trees, the animals and the fishes; quiet with the rush of the wind, the rustle of the leaves and the song of the birds; still with the flowing of the river,

the changes in the seasons and the passing of the years. I have given my life to God, the father of my Lord Christ. Him I have promised to follow, all my days.'

And then Kevin sang.

'King of the Mysteries, you existed before the elements, before the sun was set in the sky, before the waters covered the ocean floor; beautiful King, you are without beginning and without end. And you are creating women and men to care for your world, always praising you for your boundless and eternal love.'

And then Kevin blessed the herdsman.

I nuzzled against him as he led us to the lakeside, all the while fondling my neck. He took some cool, clear water, blessed it, and gave it to the herdsman, saying 'Take this. It is given for you. Go and sprinkle it upon your cattle.'

The herdsman did as he was told. Straightaway the frenzied calves became quiet and still, and their mothers licked them with love. That night our milk flowed freely and abundantly. And as I slept, I heard again the words which Kevin had first whispered in my ear by the lakeside.

'There are three slender threads on which the world swings: the thin stream of milk from a cow's udder; the thin stalk with which a blackbird weaves her nest; and the thin string of grace by which God holds us up.'

Speaking to the Emperor   Sikh.

Long before dawn a huge crowd had gathered. Everyone was shivering slightly in the cold air. Today would be an extraordinary, eventful day. Of this everyone was sure. But what exactly was going to happen? And what would it all mean? What would be the effects rippling into their lives, and into the lives of their children, and their grandchildren, and their great grandchildren? To these questions no one knew the answers.

This was the day that their young leader, Guru Hargobind, was to be released from jail, and they were waiting near the prison gates. Would he be coming out alone? Or would there be others with him? If indeed there were others, how many would there be? Or might he not come at all? Might he insist on staying inside the prison, rotting away in body and mind? To these questions also no one knew the answers.

Guru Hargobind had still been only a small child, no more than about eleven years old, when his saintly father Guru Arjan — who had composed so many beautiful hymns about his faith and love of God — had been put to death by the Emperor. But Guru Arjan's followers had readily agreed that he should be their new leader as soon as he was old enough. From the earliest days, he always carried two swords. One for fighting battles in the world, he used to say, and the other for fighting demons and fears inside the human heart and mind. . . . To the people he was a holy man, like his father before him,

but also he was worldly, he knew how to speak to the Emperor.

Guru Arjan once said: 'I do not keep the Hindu fast, nor the Muslim Ramadan, I serve Him alone who is my refuge.'

The first glints of dawn light were appearing, and the whole sky to the east was beginning to gleam and redden.

The Emperor Jahangir had become very ill and even with the best medicine that money could buy none of the palace doctors could make him better. Every day he seemed to be getting weaker and the palace was hushed and sad. At last he asked one of his officials — a jealous and ambitious man called Chandu — to send for his counsellors. Perhaps they would have some advice, some words of wisdom to impart.

It was too good a chance for Chandu to miss. He had resented Guru Hargobind for a long time — the special relationship he enjoyed with the Emperor, the hunting expeditions they used to go on together, and the way that the Emperor, himself a Muslim, often preferred his company to that of his Muslim officials. It seemed to Chandu that fate was delivering him a golden opportunity... and he must turn it to his best advantage. Taking the counsellors aside, he promised them a handsome reward if they would tell the Emperor exactly what he told them to say.

'All human help has failed you,' the counsellors explained, 'and you must seek divine aid. The best advice we can give you is to imprison a pious man in the fort of Gwalior, where he will pray constantly, from out of his suffering, for your release from this dreadful illness.'

'Those are wise words, indeed,' interjected Chandu. 'And for a holy man you need look no further than Guru Hargobind... you would do well to send him!'

The Emperor turned the proposal over in his mind. It was certainly an unusual idea... it seemed a litle unfair... there was probably something behind it, of course, though he did not know what... but on the other hand the doctors seemed to have given up hope... and, who knows, perhaps the sincere prayer of an honest man could help his recovery... and perhaps somehow the suffering and self-sacrifice of a devout Sikh could bring him back to health. In the end he agreed, and Guru Hargobind was taken to the fort.

Guru Arjan once prayed: 'You are the tree and the world is its branches... You are my Father, you are my Mother.'

The Emperor had made a miraculous recovery and had sent word that Guru Hargobind could be released, but the young leader had refused to leave prison. 'There are so many other prisoners here,' came his reply, 'and they too are imprisoned unfairly. I have grown to love them and to respect them, and I refuse now to leave them behind. I demand that they should be allowed to come out of prison with me. Otherwise I shall stay where I am, in the dark and filthy dungeons of Gwalior fort.'

The Emperor had been amazed. How dare someone address him like this? There were at that time 52 other prisoners in the fort at Gwalior, all of them Hindus. The Emperor himself was a Muslim. He could not begin to understand why Guru Hargobind cared so much about his fellow prisoners. 'But very well,' he had said. 'I will release as many prisoners as are able to hold to your cloak as you walk through the prison gates.'

What would happen? This is what the crowd wanted to know, and why they had gathered. The sun was high enough now to cast soft shadows. The prison gates opened, and Hargobind stood on the threshold. As he moved forward the crowd gasped. The cloak he was wearing was massive, massive, stretching as far the eye could see. The people at the front of the crowd began counting. Yes, every single one of the 52 Hindu prisoners was holding on to Hargobind's cloak.

Guru Arjan once sang: 'As a performing juggler acts many parts . . . so is our Creator one, the only One.'

The huge cloak billowed in the morning breeze. Guru Hargobind walked first, and behind him, but joined to him by their hands clutching the tassels on his amazing and enormous cloak, came the 52 released captives.

The sun was climbing in the sky. Guru Hargobind stepped out boldly into the morning sunlight. Where would he go now, the crowd wondered. To the temple, to pray? Or to the palace, to speak to the Emperor?

A Shady Deal

It was a lovely old tree. Its branches were flat and wide, and were covered in leaves almost all the year round. It stood close to the road, and was the ideal spot to sit and rest at noon on a hot day on your way home from work or the shops. You could just sit for a while and enjoy the cool air, or chat with friends and swap stories, and catch up with the news. Everyone loved it: it seemed like everyone's tree.

Everyone, that is, except one: there was a big house near the tree, and the owner of the house insisted that the tree was his, his alone, for the land it stood on belonged to him. Whenever he caught anyone enjoying the shade, he would shoo them away. 'Clear off! Go on! Out!' he'd yell, shaking his fist and sometimes brandishing a stick. One morning a sign appeared beside the tree:

> **PRIVATE SHADE!**
>
> **Keep Off!**
>
> **By Order.**

They'd taken his mean, horrible behaviour long enough, and this notice was the end. Who did he think he was? They weren't hurting anyone, they weren't even stopping him using it, they weren't spoiling the tree. What if he did own the land... that didn't give him the right... But all the same, what could they do? Ah, the Effendi, as they liked to call him, their local hero, would know! He'd been around, he knew the ways of the world, he could outsmart anyone.

The Effendi studied the situation and noticed something interesting which gave him an idea: the shade moved with the sun and the moon, covering the road in the day, the land-owner's courtyard in the evening and the whole roof of his house at night. The Effendi talked to everyone who liked to use the tree to see what they thought, and together they drew up a plan to ensure that they could still have the shade without being harassed — and could teach you-know-who a lesson into the bargain. It would cost, though. But everyone chipped in, and they collected four hundred dollars. Then the Effendi went and sat under the tree himself. Sure enough, before long out stomped the landowner, shouting, 'Clear off! Go on! Out!'

'I beg your pardon,' replied the Effendi politely. 'Surely this is common land and the road belongs to everyone. Why can't I just rest here for a while?'

'That's as may be, but you're sitting in the shade of my tree. People can only enjoy the shade of my tree if they can afford it.'

The Effendi questioned him with great interest. 'Do you mean the shade is for sale? If so, I'll make you an offer you can't refuse.'

'Don't talk big!' retorted the landowner. 'You couldn't afford my prices!'

'Is four hundred dollars big enough?'

'Now you're talking. But let me see the colour of your money!'

'I'll go one better,' the Effendi proposed. 'Let's make this all legal and above board.'

So off he went to a lawyer, had an agreement properly drawn up, and signed in the presence of witnesses.

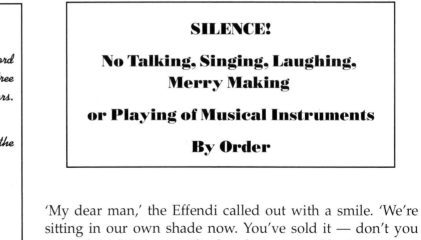

Agreement

Let it be known that the shade from the tree beside the house of H. I. Lord is hereby handed over to E. F. Fend. D.I.Y., until such time as the tree withers and dies, upon payment of the sum of 400 (four hundred) dollars. This agreement is binding upon both parties and cannot be revoked.

The parties to the agreement have signed and fixed their seal in the presence of witnesses.

------------------ H. I. Lord

------------------ E.F. Fend, D. I. Y.

------------------ A. Law (Commissioner of Oaths)

------------------ B. Case (Witness)

------------------ C. Court (Witness)

Receipt

Received from E. F. Fend, D. I. Y., the sum of 400 (four hundred) dollars as payment for the use of shade from tree on my land near the road, until such time as the tree withers and dies.

H. I. Lord

The next day people gathered under the tree, and were relaxed and happy once more. They laughed and sang, and hadn't a care in the world, until the landowner strode across to complain about the noise. He put up another notice:

SILENCE!

No Talking, Singing, Laughing, Merry Making

or Playing of Musical Instruments

By Order

'My dear man,' the Effendi called out with a smile. 'We're sitting in our own shade now. You've sold it — don't you remember? We can surely do whatever we like in our own shade.' The landowner had nothing to say, and stalked off, muttering to himself.

Early one evening, a few days later, when the landlord was taking the cool air in his courtyard, the Effendi strolled in with his donkey. 'Clear off! Go on! Out!'

'Whatever do you mean?' enquired the Effendi calmly. 'I only followed the shade in here. I think you'll find I'm perfectly within my rights.'

The following week, some of the landowner's wealthy friends arrived and sat down under the tree to have a drink with him. 'Excuse me,' the Effendi politely pointed out, 'but you cannot occupy this shade, I am sorry. It does not belong to this gentleman, you see.' Without a word they got up and left, leaving their host beside himself with embarrassment.

The selling of shade — unheard of anywhere — soon became news all around, and the story made the front page of the local paper.

COOL PLAN FOR LOCAL HOT SPOT

And in a light-hearted, carefree mood, some of the shade regulars made up a song, and popped it through the land-owner's letter-box.

When the heat was too fierce on a hot
scorching day
And we needed a place for basking,
The Effendi thought hard and thought
of a way,
And won for us what we were asking.

He did it right, he played it cool,
He made the tyrant look a fool.

One night, the landowner woke up and saw the Effendi with friends on the roof of his house, joking and playing music. Storming out, he screamed, 'Clear off! Go on! Out!'

'We're in the shade we bought,' the Effendi answered court-eously.

'I didn't sell you the shade of the moon,' the landowner raged.

'My dear man,' the Effendi explained, 'our agreement didn't say anything about the source of the light and the shade. Perhaps you ought to have studied the terms more carefully.'

Soon afterwards the landowner moved out. And then another sign appeared:

FOR SALE OR RENT ON EXCELLENT TERMS

Luxury mansion, all mod cons.

Sitting Tenants in Shade

The Football Match

One day God came down from heaven. She went to a football match. It was an important match between Christians and Muslims.

For the first half God dressed herself with the scarf, colours, cap and emblems of the Christian supporters. She stood on the Christian terraces. Three times during the first half the Muslims scored a goal, and on each occasion the Christian supporters stood there silent, and very sad and forsaken. God, however, leapt and shouted and waved with delight. The Christian supporters nearby were angry with her, but thought she must be completely mad, and didn't do anything to her.

For the second half God dressed herself with the scarf, colours, cap and emblems of the Muslim supporters. She stood on the Muslim terraces. Three times during the second half the Christians scored a goal, and on each occasion the Muslim supporters stood there silent, and very sad and forsaken. God, however, leapt and shouted and waved with delight. The Muslims supporters nearby were angry with her, but thought she must be completely mad, and didn't do anything to her.

In an amusement arcade after the match some Christian and some Muslim supporters happened to meet. God was in there too, playing on one of the machines, and wearing now both sets of scarves, colours, caps and emblems. The Christian and the Muslim supporters talked to each other about her, and told each other they thought she was absolutely mad.

'I wonder,' said one of the supporters, 'what on earth she thinks she's playing at.'

Two Kinds of Idiot

The sun was warm, and she was quietly enjoying her snack lunch in the park near her office. She only had half an hour off from her job as a secretary in one of the nearby office blocks, and was savouring these moments of freedom. Her peace and quiet were brutally shattered, however, by four young men who suddenly appeared before her.

'How about a taste of your cheese roll?' asked the first. 'Can I lick your ice-cream, miss?' said the second. 'Give us a bite of yer banana, love,' said the third. 'I wouldn't mind sipping some of your low-calorie coca cola,' said the fourth.

'Who are you?' she asked the first.

'I'm someone who's homeless,' he said.

'There are only two kinds of homeless creature in this world,' she replied. 'Which kind are you?' He couldn't reply.

'Since you can't reply,' she said, 'I'm not going to help you.' Then she spoke to the second. 'Who are you?' she asked.

'I'm a drop-out,' he said.

'There are only two kinds of drop-out in this world,' she replied. 'Which kind of drop-out are you?' He couldn't reply. 'Since you can't reply,' she said, 'I'm not going to help you.'

Then she spoke to the third. 'Who are you?' she asked.

'I'm someone who's poor and oppressed,' he said.

'There are only two kinds of poor and oppressed creature in this world,' she replied. 'Which kind are you?' He couldn't reply. 'Since you can't reply,' she said, 'I'm not going to help you.'

Finally she spoke to the fourth. 'Who are you?' she asked.

'Me? I'm just an idiot,' he said.

'There are only two kinds of idiot in this world,' she replied. 'Which kind are you?' He couldn't reply. 'Since you can't reply,' she said, 'I'm not going to help you.'

She finished her lunch. But then she felt a little sorry for the four young men, and she invited them back to her firm's offices, and bought them all something to eat from a snack machine in one of the corridors. She remembered that her boss was out for the afternoon, and she took the four men into her boss' room to eat their snacks.

But alas! Her boss wasn't out for the afternoon after all, and he came back and found the four young men lounging around in his office, and talking with his secretary. He was furious. 'How dare you bring a collection of your layabout boyfriends in here?' he shouted. 'How dare you?' He arranged immediately for her to appear before the senior personnel manager.

She told the personnel manager her story. 'These four men approached me in the park, claiming that they wanted help. I felt I did want to help them, and that I ought to, but that it wouldn't be right to help them in the way they asked. So I asked each of them a question. They couldn't answer my questions, so — so, well, so, I decided to buy them all a snack lunch back here at the office. After all, this firm gives a lot of money to charity, and senior managers are always saying we ought to be socially responsible, and be aware of the Third World, and so on. I was just doing my bit. I didn't think anyone would object.'

The personnel manager asked her what the four questions had been, and she told him. He was extremely mystified, and asked her to explain.

'There are only two kinds of homeless creature in this world,' she said, 'and they're the sun and the moon. There are only two kinds of drop-out, and they're autumn leaves and cigarette ends. There are only two kinds of poor and oppressed creature, and they're stray dogs and — '

'Yes?'

'Secretaries.'

'I see,' said the personnel manager. 'And you're going to tell me that there are only two kinds of idiot?'

'Yes.'

'And what are they?'

'You won't be angry if I tell you?'

'I can't say.'

'I'll tell you anyway. One kind of idiot is like my boss, who jumps to conclusions without trying to find out the truth. And the other kind of idiot in this world is like you, sir, who doesn't even know what truth is.'

He wasn't angry.

Draupadi's Prayer Hindu

Draupadi was the wife of Prince Yuddhishthira. He was one of the noblest, bravest, finest rulers our world has ever known.

But alas, he loved the risks of gambling. Most of all he was excited when playing with dice.

One fateful day, he played dice against his arch enemy Duryodhana.

He staked his favourite jewels, and lost. He staked all his horses in order to try to win back the jewels, and lost. Then he staked his palace in order to try to win back his horses and his jewels, and lost. He staked his whole army, in order to try to win back his horses, jewels and palace, and lost. He staked himself and his four brothers, and lost. Finally, in the hope of winning everything back, he staked Draupadi his wife. He lost.

Duryodhana was delighted and excited to have the beautiful Draupadi under his complete control and power. Exulting in his victory, he decided that he would undress her in full view of all the men in his palace, and in full sight also of Yuddhishthira and his brothers. To cause her to stand naked and helpless in front of all his courtiers and principal supporters, totally and utterly dependent on his own whims, wishes and desires, would be the climax of his triumph.

As Duryodhana approached to tear away her sari, Draupadi began to pray to the Lord Krishna. At the same time she held on to her clothes with tightly clenched fists. Duryodhana struggled with her, slapped her, shook her, and was slowly prising her fingers away from the silk of her dress. She realised that she needed to pray even more earnestly and fervently. Letting go of her covering, she raised her hands, loose now and relaxed, in entreaty and surrender. 'O Lord of my heart,' she prayed, 'O Boatman of my life, may your will only be fulfilled.'

It was at that precise moment that the miracle happened. Draupadi's sari became suddenly endless and inexhaustible. Duryodhana pulled on it, and pulled it away from her. But however much silk he pulled away, Draupadi remained fully clothed. Eventually, with all his courtiers watching, he had to admit that Draupadi was for ever beyond him.

It was at a different time and in a different place that Krishna once said to Arjuna, one of Yuddhishthira's four brothers: 'I am the waves of the sea, and the leaves of the trees. In my hand I hold the stars of the skies, like pearls in a necklace. I am heat, and I am ice. I am the wind, and all the earth.'

The Door   Buddhist

It was so unfair, so terribly, terribly unfair.

She could scarcely believe it. That they dared do this to her. That they did not see her as a full human being, but treated her as if she were a dirty scruffy scrap of paper, to be thrown away. She was bitter and she was totally, in every cell and muscle of her being, determined. She would get even, would get the wrong righted, would get justice.

There was a belief in her land that justice was available to you if you stood outside a certain door at the back of the king's palace. Every now and again, it was said, the king personally would come to this door, and open it, and invite you inside if you were waiting there for justice, and if he already knew that your case was just.

There was no record of anyone ever having been actually invited inside the palace in this way. But then, no one had ever waited outside the door for more than a few days.

No one knew for certain that the king would indeed come. Some said that he came to the door no more than once every hundred years, but only one time in every thousand visits to the door did he actually open it.

She would stay at the door, she resolved, for as long as necessary. If the king never came, so be it: she would stay at the palace door until her death.

And so it was. She stood for day after day, week after week, month after month, year after year, outside the insignificant little door at the back of the palace. Everyone in the country knew that she was there, and every day people would come to stare at her, and to shake their heads in amazement, that she was so persistent. In the course of time they began speaking to her, and asking her advice.

In particular they asked her advice about justice and fairness in their own personal lives, and they asked advice on how they could live without bitterness in their own hearts. Her advice was always very beautiful, and very wise. Always there was a crowd around her, waiting patiently for her wise advice. People would wait for days and days, just in order to consult her. And they would sleep there on the open ground near to her, waiting, waiting, for the advice she would give them.

Ten, twenty, thirty, forty, fifty years passed. One starlit night she was standing as usual with her back to the door. All around her on the ground there were people sleeping, hundreds on hundreds of them waiting to ask for her advice. Behind her she heard the door of the palace open, and a voice whispered, 'Enter, my child, enter, your patience is rewarded, you shall have justice, enter, you need no longer to stand waiting, come into my palace for the rest of your life.'

She looked at all the people round about, lying there asleep, waiting to consult her. Could she abandon them? Behind her the voice spoke again, 'Enter, my child, enter my palace for the rest of your life.' She looked out at all the people waiting for her, depending on her.

She did not move. Behind her, she heard the door softly close.

In the Bag

If you're a magician, and if you have a magic bag, is there anything at all that you cannot do? I don't know, but that's the question this story is about.

A new priest came to work in a certain North African town, many centuries ago. He said the only way to get to heaven was by going to his church. The town's magician didn't like this at all. He argued with the priest, but the priest insisted, 'You can't get to heaven except by going to church.'

'So you're saying that you're the only person in this town who can determine people's eternal destiny?' asked the magician.

'Well I wouldn't put it exactly like that,' said the priest. 'Only God can determine people's eternal destiny.'

'Only priests can cause miracles to happen?'

'No, only God can do that.'

'Look at this bag I've got. Do you believe that this bag can cause miracles to happen?'

'No, of course I don't believe anything so absurd.'

'Would you object if I asked this bag to swallow you up?'

'I'd think you were a bit mad, but obviously I wouldn't object, since I know perfectly well that you're talking nonsense.'

'I see,' said the magician. Then turning to his bag he said 'Swallow this priest!', and that's precisely what the bag did, and the priest was never seen again.

A new priest came to the town. The magician had the same conversation with him, and used his magic bag to get rid of him. It was the same with the next priest, and the next, and the next. But eventually a priest arrived who said he was happy to acknowledge that the magician's bag could swallow things and people up. The two of them made a deal. The priest would concentrate on preaching sermons and running the church, and the magician would concentrate on removing evil people and unpleasant experiences, by putting them all into his magic bag to be swallowed up. This arrangement worked very well for many years.

Eventually it was time for the magician to die. He found himself at the gates of Hell. 'But this isn't right,' he said. 'I shouldn't be here. I've spent my life getting rid of unpleasant things and evil people, by putting them in my magic bag.' The receptionist in Hell consulted the magician's files. 'It says here,' she explained, 'that you've been sent to Hell because you spent so much of your life thinking about bad people and unpleasant experiences. You have more in common with people here than with people in Heaven.'

'What absolute nonsense,' said the magician, and he put Hell into his bag, and Hell ceased to exist. He then took himself to the gates of Heaven. The angel working in reception pointed that he wasn't expected, and said he couldn't come in. 'There's nowhere else for me to go,' said the magician, 'since Hell doesn't exist any more. Anyway, I can easily put Heaven in my bag too if you're not careful. The fact is, you haven't really got a choice.'

So the angel let the magician into Heaven. He has lived there happily ever since. Or so, anyway, said a certain priest. But he said it with a twinkle in his eye, and perhaps he was joking.

If you're a magician, and if you have a magic bag, is there anything at all that you cannot do? I don't know, but that's the question this story is about.

ORGANISING

The Stonecutter

Once upon a time, thousands of years ago in ancient China, there was a stonecutter. He was a very irritable and bitter person, always complaining about his bad luck.

One day he walked past the mansion of a rich merchant, and as usual began complaining. As he glanced at the fine carriages in the courtyard, and saw all the important people standing around, he was bitter with envy. 'How wonderful and powerful that man is,' he thought. 'I wish I could be like that! Then I wouldn't have to spend all my time cutting and shaping stone.'

To his enormous surprise, he suddenly found himself transformed into a rich merchant. He had great wealth and power, and was surrounded by luxury. But one day he saw a very important official from the government going past his house, surrounded by attendants and escorted by troops of soldiers. As the procession went down the street everyone in the city bowed low in respect. 'Oh if only I could be a government official, with everyone respecting me,' thought the man. 'That would be much better than being a mere merchant. I could really make things happen.'

At that moment he was transformed into a government official. He was carried everywhere in a handsome sedan chair, and all the people of the city bowed down to him. But the summer weather that year was particularly hot and uncomfortable. From his sticky sedan chair the man looked up and watched the sun high in the sky. It shone there so proudly, totally unaffected by anything else. 'Oh if only I could be the sun,' thought the man. 'Then I wouldn't be sticky and uncomfortable, nothing would stop me from being still and contented.'

At that moment he was transformed into the sun. He shone down fiercely onto the countryside, and was delighted that many people cursed him for scorching their crops. But a dark grey cloud moved between himself and the earth, and his light was no longer able to reach the land below. 'How very powerful that cloud is,' he thought. 'If only I could be a cloud. I wouldn't be thwarted then by other things.'

He was transformed into a rain cloud, and he took great pleasure in causing floods all over the country. But one day he found himself being blown all over the place by a forceful wind. 'Oh if only I could be the wind!' he thought. 'Then

I could really throw my weight around. I could move, push, compel, force; I could do anything.'

He was transformed into the wind, and he roared and blew and moved all manner of things from one place to another. But one day he came up against something which would not shift however strongly he blew. It was a great towering rock. 'Oh, if only I could be that rock, unmovable,' he thought. 'Then absolutely nothing could push me around, nothing could have any impact on me.'

He was transformed into a great rock, and felt immensely strong, powerful, unmovable. But then he heard the knock, knock, knock of a hammer hitting a chisel, and he realised with terror that he was himself being chipped away.

'So there is someone or something more powerful even than a towering rock,' he thought. 'Who or what on earth can it be?' He looked down. At the base of the towering rock, like a mere tiny insect, he could see a man with a hammer and chisel, chipping, breaking, shaping, carving.

It was a stonecutter.

Means and Ends Jewish

The floods were unexpected and it was all systems go to save the community before the waters engulfed the valley. One family was trapped in their home and neighbours urged them to escape with them in their cart. 'We have trust in God,' the father called from the window. 'Don't be afraid. He'll save you, too. We're not moving.'

The waters rose quickly and they were forced upstairs. A passing boatman beckoned to them. 'Our faith will not waver,' replied the mother. 'Peace be with you!'

Finally, on the roof of their home, refusing to catch hold of a lowered rope ladder, they waved the helicopter off and the children chorused, 'We have believed in God all our lives. God will not let us down.'

Shoulder to shoulder, they faced the Almighty, with heavy hearts and harsh voices. 'How could you! We have been your faithful servants — surely we deserved better! Why didn't you help us?'

'But I did,' said God. 'I sent you the neighbours with the cart. I sent you the boat. I sent you the helicopter.'

Just the Ticket Jewish

'Dear God,' he prayed, 'let me win the lottery this week. Times are bad. We are all starving and the children need new shoes. Please help, amen.'

'Dear God,' he prayed again, 'we didn't win the lottery, as you know. I can't believe that you'd let me down. Things have got a lot worse. We haven't eaten now for days, the baby is really ill and we'll lose the house if I don't get some money soon. Please help, amen.'

'Dear God,' he prayed once more, 'I don't understand at all. Two weeks have passed since I first prayed to you, and still we haven't won. We are faint with hunger and exhausted from worry. The bailiffs will be here tomorrow if I can't pay the rent and then what will become of us? I'm begging you now — I'll never ask for anything again! Please help, amen.'

'Meet me half way,' came the reply. 'Buy a ticket.'

God Willing

The Mother Superior was getting anxious, and this surprised all the sisters in the convent, for normally she was very serene and untroubled. Normally, there was nothing that could rattle this very devout and holy person.

The problem was to do with the convent's minibus. One of its sidelights needed fixing, and the Mother Superior had sent it to a small garage close to the convent. The minibus had been taken in on Monday, with a message that the matter was very urgent. The mechanic had been very respectful and reassuring — 'yes certainly, certainly, Mother, everything will be all right. God willing, you shall have the bus back tomorrow.'

But on Tuesday the minibus was not ready. Merely the same message came — 'certainly, certainly, Mother, everything will be all right. God willing, you shall have the bus back tomorrow.' And again it happened on Wednesday. The bus wasn't ready, but the same message came — 'certainly, certainly, Mother, everything will be all right. God willing, you shall have the bus back tomorrow.'

And yet again on Thursday — 'certainly, certainly, Mother, everything will be all right. God willing, you shall have the bus back tomorrow.'

The Mother Superior sent two sisters down to the garage. 'Tell the mechanic that I sent you,' she told them very firmly, 'and ask him a question from me.'

The sisters couldn't tell whether the Mother Superior was angry.

'Ask him if he thinks it would help to leave God out of it. And tell him I'm very keen to know his answer.'

Say No More

The holy woman of the village was used to requests for advice but it came as something of a surprise when a young man came to her for material help.

'I'm getting married very soon, and I haven't got anything,' he explained. 'Nowhere to live, no cooker, no furniture, nothing. If you could arrange a little flat for us with all the basics, that would be marvellous. Of course a few extras would go down well, I won't deny that — a fridge, a TV (preferably with remote control, please), a microwave, a jacuzzi, a CD player — you know the kind of thing.'

'Say no more!' said the holy woman. 'Take this incense and when the moon is full go to the marble house with seven palm trees in front. Knock three times and the door will open. Lower your head and go inside. There, on a low brass table covered with a red cloth, you will see a blue teapot. If you light the incense before it, a jinn will appear. Put your request to her.'

When the moon was full, the young man took the incense and went to the marble house with the seven palm trees in front. He knocked three times and the door opened. He lowered his head and went inside. There, on a low brass table covered with a red cloth, he saw a blue teapot. He lit the incense before it and a jinn appeared. He put his request to her.

'I'm getting married very soon, and I haven't got anything,' he explained. 'Nowhere to live, no cooker, no furniture, nothing. If you could arrange a little flat for us with all the basics, that would be marvellous. Of course a few extras would go down well, I won't deny that — a fridge, a TV (preferably with remote control, please), a microwave, a jacuzzi, a CD player — you know the kind of thing.'

'If I could get all that for you,' said the jinn, ' do you think I'd be stuck here in this grotty little teapot?'

A Double Life   *Jewish*

It was a very special season of the year when the traveller arrived — that awesome time before the High Holy Days in autumn. He would stay for a brief while, he thought, and join the pious little community each day in their early morning prayers. It was no good being on the road now: he needed this chance to reflect on the year that had passed, and to take stock of his soul, and to renew himself once more. But that is never easy. It would do him good to be with other Jews, to hear with them early each morning the blowing of the ram's horn, the call to spiritual awakening.

Why was the rabbi never there, though, he wondered. They had a rabbi for sure: he'd be out and about in the day in his long dark coat and broad-rimmed hat. He'd be teaching in the evening. But he was never in the synagogue for dawn prayers! What kind of a rabbi was that? But whenever he asked, 'Where's the rabbi?' he'd be told quite bluntly, 'The rabbi's in heaven!' What could that possibly mean? Was the rabbi still asleep, dreaming of heaven? Was it some kind of cover-up? What on earth could the rabbi be up to?

One evening, after a study-session at the rabbi's house, he couldn't bear not knowing any longer. So when everyone else got up to leave, he crawled under the rabbi's bed without being noticed and hid there all night, keeping watch, determined to see exactly what it was that the rabbi did.

Before it was light, the call to prayer rang out. Above his head the rabbi's bed creaked and he thought he heard him sigh. There was movement in the house of people getting up. There were voices on the stairs. There were footsteps in the street. Then all was quiet and still.

Moonlight shone through the window, and two feet appeared over the edge of the bed. The rabbi stretched and yawned and crossed the room to a cupboard. He took out what seemed to be a pair of woollen trousers, a rough jacket, a wide belt, a felt hat, and high leather boots. One by one, he put them on. And then from the kitchen he got a length of rope and . . . an axe! He coiled the rope round his shoulder, shoved the axe into his belt and stepped out into the cold, damp air.

The traveller's heart was thumping — he didn't like the look of it at all — but curiosity overcame him and he felt impelled to follow at a safe distance. Walking in the shadows, the rabbi wended his way through the narrow streets and out of the town into the wood. In a clearing, he stopped by a small tree, pulled out the axe, and . . . thwack! He struck the tree again and again until it snapped and fell. Then he deftly chopped the tree into logs, and the logs into splints. He tied the splints into a bundle, slung it on his back, and headed back for the town.

He came to a tumble-down house in one of the backstreets and gently tapped on the window. 'Who's there?' came a frightened woman's voice.

'I'm selling wood — for next to nothing.' With that, he pushed the door and went inside. The room was sparsely furnished and, even in the grey light of early morning, it looked very shabby. A frail old woman lay in bed. 'I'm a poor widow: where would I ever get money for wood?'

'I'll give you ten pence worth on credit.'

'But I could never repay you,' she replied.

'I'm willing to trust you with a bundle of wood because I know that you'll pay me one day when you can.'

'Thank you, but I can't even get up out of bed, let alone light a fire.'

The rabbi laid the wood in the stove, and as he did so he softly said the first part of the special morning prayers. As he lit the wood, he said the second part. The fire crackled brightly, and he said the third part.

He left without waiting to be thanked. Dawn was breaking now as he hurried back to his house and as the last blast of the ram's horn pierced the air. The congregation was pouring out of the synagogue into the morning light, and the rabbi quickened his step. He arrived home breathless, just in time to change into his black coat and broad-brimmed hat, comb his beard, and compose himself at the table, with an open book before him. Moments later, his followers arrived for morning study and he was ready with a smile.

The traveller stayed right through the High Holy Days, and eventually made his home in that community. In later years there were other visitors at that season, and they would ask during the dawn prayers, as he had done, 'Where's the rabbi?' They were told, as he had been, 'The rabbi's in heaven!'

And he would always add, 'If not higher . . .'

I'm Staying Here Buddhist

Once there were three sisters.

When they were grown up each decided to seek truth and purpose in her own way. The first declared : 'I'm going to look after the sick and broken, the streets are full of them, I will bring them healing and care.' The second : 'Everywhere I see people in dispute and conflict with one another. I will go out to reconcile them, I will bring them peace.' The third sister declared that she would stay at home.

After two years the first two sisters returned. The first said: 'It's hopeless, there are simply too many sick people, I cannot cope.' The second said much the same: 'It's impossible, I'm torn to shreds.' They sat in exhausted and burnt-out despair, looking at each other.

Then the third sister filled a bowl with muddy water from a nearby pool. 'Look into that,' she said. 'Look.'

They looked but saw nothing, only muddy water. 'Let it stand,' she said. 'Let it be.'

After a while they looked again. The water was clear now, and they saw their own reflections in it, as clearly as in a mirror.

The third sister told them : 'When the water is stirred up it is muddy and you can see nothing. It is clear only when it is very still. It is the same with us human beings. You can see clearly only when you are still, very still. Only when in stillness you see your own self can you see also what you should do, where you should go.

'Only then can you have hope and faith in the future, and in the worthwhileness of political endeavour, and in your own giftedness, grace and creativity.

'Only then can you plunge, with passionate love, into caring for others, whether through medicine or through politics.

'Only then can you be indifferent to rewards, indifferent to the fruits of action.'

The Way To Go Buddhist

Every single blade tickled his toes and every single pebble pressed into the soles of his feet, as he stepped slowly and mindfully along the stony path through the fields. It was an important journey for a young monk to be making and he was humbled by the task. He struggled within himself against the urge to quicken his pace for he was on his way to help the villagers build a temple — and he was keen to do it. Yet he must not rush, for every moment holds its own reality and everything is in the Now.

The day wore on, the grass and stones began to feel the same and his mind started to wander. To build a temple . . . to build a temple . . . what could be more Buddha-like? There the villagers could meditate on their way to enlightenment and his first sermon would be on the need to purify the mind. His thoughts drifted to the sermon on compassion for others which the Buddha had given some 2,500 years before on a similar occasion . . . or rather, the sermon the Buddha had started to give. Noticing how the people had fidgeted and yawned, the Buddha realised how hungry they were: he had tried to feed their minds but it was their bodies that really needed food. So with an open heart he had shared his meal with them all...

The day began to drag and his feet grew weary. If only there were a better route to the village, he thought. Those poor people! How hard it must be for them to travel if they have to walk this way — and how hard for others to come to them. They really need a proper made-up road. Still, he reminded himself, the temple will be a peaceful place for them to meditate on their way to enlightenment. . . But how will they share it with others and how will they feel compassion for those in the world they will never know?

Dusk was falling as he reached his destination. Excited villagers rushed to greet him, falling to the ground to touch his dusty, swollen feet.

'Welcome!' they cried. 'You have come to build our temple!'

'Yes,' he answered, 'I have come to build a road!'

Calm in a Teacup   Jewish

They had been sitting there for
almost ages, not speaking, not moving,
perhaps not even thinking, each staring
deeply into their own cup. Finally
the silence and the spell
were broken by a heavy
sigh. 'Life is like
a cup of tea.'

'Whatever do you mean?' 'I don't know. What do you think I am?
— a philosopher?'

Is There Anybody There?

Jewish

It had all happened so quickly — you have to be so careful . . . one minute he was walking along the edge of the cliff, minding his own business, and the next he was half-way down, suspended over the rocks and the raging sea by his trouser pocket hooked onto a branch.

He felt the fabric begin to weaken. . . A few more stitches snapped. The crashing waters below — and certain death — seemed to be getting nearer. . .

'Help! Is there anybody there?' he cried out in anguish and despair. 'Please, please,' he called again.

And then, as though from far away, a voice spoke. 'Do not hold on. Release the fabric from the twig and let go. Trust me. You will float gently downwards, like a feather in the breeze, and you will land softly on a smooth rock. The waters will lap against your feet, soothing your every ache, loosening your every tension. . .'

'Is there anybody else there?' he called.

Paradise Gardens   Muslim

There was once a civil servant who was feeling totally fed up with the work he had to do. He sat at his desk in Whitehall, and looked with disgust and nausea at the piles of paperwork in front of him. His work was a treadmill of one dreary and pointless chore after another. He felt like a key on a keyboard, a scrap of paper in a file, a misprint on a spreadsheet.

He mentioned his feelings one day to someone on the train, as he was travelling to work. 'We all feel like that, though, don't we,' said this other person. 'We're all condemned to pointless and dreary drudgery, aren't we? It all goes back to Adam in the Garden of Eden. He disobeyed instructions, and ever since then human beings have had to slave away at pointless chores. It's tough, but there's nothing anyone can do about it.'

'If only,' said the civil servant, 'I could get my hands on old Father Adam. I — I feel I'd like to dig up his grave and dance on the blighter's bones . . or find his files, and shred the lot . . . or burn all the books he ever wrote, if he did write any . . . I really hate that man.'

Now it so happened that God was listening to this conversation, and he decided to try and help. He sent an angel, disguised as an ordinary human being, to have a word with the civil servant.

'I absolutely hate my work, ' explained the civil servant. 'I feel I'd like to dig up old Father Adam's grave and dance on his bones.'

'Mm,' said the angel, 'that wouldn't really help, you know. But I can arrange, if you like, for you to go and live in a wonderful place which I know, and you'll have there a life of complete leisure. You'll never have to do a stroke of work if you decide to live there.'

'It sounds wonderful,' replied the civil servant. 'When can I start?'

'Straightaway,' said the angel. 'The place is called the Paradise Gardens Theme Park. You can live there in complete luxury and leisure, but on one condition: you mustn't speak to anyone else whom you happen to meet there.'

'Well that's perfectly all right by me,' commented the man. 'To be frank, I don't much care for other people anyway. Let's start.'

And immediately the civil servant found himself in the Paradise Gardens Theme Park. He lived in wonderful leisure. But one day, after he had been there for about a week, he saw a gardener pruning rose bushes. The gardener was cutting out the fresh green shoots bearing buds and throwing these away, and he was leaving all the dead wood from previous years. The civil servant wondered what to do. 'Do I speak, or do I keep silent?' he asked himself. He was silent for a while, but eventually was seized with impatience. 'Hey,' he said to the gardener. 'Don't you realise that that's not the way to prune roses?' The gardener looked at him, and said, 'How long have you been here?' and at that moment the civil servant was transported suddenly back to his office in Whitehall. The angel was waiting for him there.

'Oh please,' begged the civil servant, 'give me another chance.'

'Very well,' said the angel, 'one more chance.' And immediately the civil servant found himself back in the Paradise Gardens Theme Park. Again he lived in wonderful leisure. But one day, after he had been there for about a week, he saw two old age pensioners chasing after a beautiful white horse. The horse was very swift as well as very graceful, and there was absolutely no chance that the pensioners could catch it. The civil servant wondered what to do. 'Do I speak, or do I keep silent?' he asked himself. He was silent for a while, but eventually was seized with impatience. 'Hey,' he said to the two old age pensioners. 'Don't you realise that you don't stand the slightest chance of catching that horse?' The old people looked at him, and said, 'How long have you been here?' and at that moment the civil servant was transported suddenly back to his office in Whitehall. The angel was waiting for him there.

'Oh please,' begged the civil servant, 'give me another chance.'

'All right,' said the angel, though very reluctantly, 'one more chance.' And immediately the civil servant found himself once more in the Paradise Gardens Theme Park. Again he lived in wonderful leisure. But one day, after he had been there for about a week, he saw four strong young men trying to lift a large heavy wheel, of the kind used in the roundabouts on the fairground. They were all standing very close to each other, and there was absolutely no possibility of lifting the wheel off the ground unless they spaced themselves out all round it. The civil servant wondered what to do. 'Do I speak, or do I keep silent?' he asked himself. He was silent for a while, but eventually was seized with impatience. 'Hey,' he said to the four strong young men. 'Don't you realise that you don't stand the slightest chance of lifting that wheel, unless you space yourselves evenly all round it?' The four men looked at him, and said, 'How long have you been here?' At that moment the civil servant was transported suddenly back to his office in Whitehall. The angel was waiting for him there.

'Oh please,' begged the civil servant, 'give me — '.

'No,' interrupted the angel. 'No more chances. Adam was only given one chance, you know, and you've had three. Three times now you have disobeyed instructions. There's nothing more I can do for you. It's tough, I know, but good-bye.'

The civil servant looked sadly at the papers on the desk before him. Pruning roses, chasing after horses, lifting a wheel . . . he had these strange memories. He sighed, and reaching forward he picked up a paper from his desk.

Standing Up and Sitting Down

Once upon a time a powerful king sat on the throne. He was tired of having to listen to his official advisers, tired of having to act wisely and sensibly, tired of having to do what was expected of him. 'If I am king,' he said to himself, 'I can do and I can say and I can be whatever I like without taking notice of anyone else.' But there was just one problem: how could he get rid of his official advisers?

Now there were some clever and ambitious young men in his kingdom and the king called them to the palace. They stood before him, and he addressed them: 'You're all sons of my official advisers. You're all strong, capable and independent. You could all be helping me to govern this country. Why do you always listen to your fathers? Wouldn't you rather be my official advisers yourselves?' He paused. 'Why not,' he went on, ' bring forward the day of your fathers' death?'

Every single one of the young men was eager to become an official adviser to the king, and to help him to govern the country. Every single one was tempted by the prospect of wealth and power. Every single one was convinced that the elders' deaths would be for the better. Every single one killed his own father.

Every single one — except one. As he stood over his father, with a knife in his hand, his father cried out, 'Didn't you sit on my knee when you were a little boy? Didn't we stand together on the river bank and watch the water rushing by? Come, sit beside me now, and let us talk. You never know when you might need me, and when I will be good for you.' The young man could not bring himself to kill his own flesh and blood, and instead hid his father far away. Then he went to join the others as official advisers at the court.

The king was pleased with the new arrangement for a while, but soon the young men began to act the way their fathers had done. The king grew tired of having to listen to the advice of the official advisers, tired of having to act wisely and sensibly, tired of having to do what was expected of him. 'If I am king,' he said to himself, 'I can do and I can say and I can be whatever I like without taking notice of anyone else.'

This time he decided to solve the problem another way and he called the young men to his chamber. They all stood in front of him and this is what he said: 'I would like a new wing in my palace, one which is quite different from any other building in the world. My instructions are, therefore, that it be built from the top downwards. I expect each one of you to begin construction tomorrow — on pain of death.'

The young men were both mystified and mortified. They sat in despair, with their heads in their hands, wondering how they could possibly start with the highest point on the roof and end up on the ground.

Only one of them had hope: that night he went to the spot where he had hidden his father. They sat and talked, and by the next morning the young man knew what to do. He stood in front of the king and said, 'Your Royal Highness, we are ready to begin building according to your instructions. Please accept the honour, as king of the land, of laying the foundation stone!'

The king stood and laughed. He laughed so much that he had to sit down. For the first time in his life, someone actually understood him, someone showed true wisdom, someone seemed to know what life was really about. The young man confessed that he had never killed his father, and that it was his father who had given him this sound advice.

The king went with the young man to the spot where his father was hiding. He stood before him and this is what he said: 'I will restore your standing in the community and you alone will guide me from now on. I see now that wisdom comes with age and the rich experience of life, for your son has told me what you said last night: "What an old man can see sitting down, a young man cannot even see standing up!"'

The Needle ~Sikh~

Most Noble and Respected Guru,

It is with the utmost humility that I write to express my most profound gratitude to You for gracing with Your presence the banquet held in Your honour at my home yesterday.

It was in the light which You Yourself shed over the entire company that the marble floors gleamed, the silken saris shimmered and the jewels shone, beyond all imagining. Even the dishes had a flavour and an aroma that the finest cooks in all India could never have created, and the minstrels played with an intensity and sweetness never heard before. Truly I was the envy of everyone in Lahore, and I felt so very proud of my riches and wealth.

I am moved to say, however, that Your parting gesture came as no small surprise to me at the time. When I thanked You in person, offering in all sincerity to give You any of my possessions which your heart desired, You did not ask for riches — though the coffers of my bank were Yours for the asking.

'Guru Nanak has handed me this tiny needle,' I told my wife. The needle lies before me even as I pen this letter. 'He has asked me to keep it safe, and return it to Him when we meet again in the next world.' I was touched by the trust You placed in me, but wondered what You meant by it. My wife, however, understood immediately, and she delighted in what You had done. So it was that she told me to run after You and ask how I could possibly take a needle with me when I die.

You did not reply directly, but You held me in Your gaze and asked me a question which I could neither answer nor escape answering. Your words still ring in my ears and I know they will never leave me. 'If you cannot take a tiny needle from this world to the next', you said, 'how on earth will you take all your wealth?'

At that very moment I saw what a waste my life has been, and that I have been selfish, greedy and mean. I have spent years in gaining and getting things which I can never keep, and have forsaken the chance of doing anything that would really last.

We talked though the night, my wife and I, and vowed that from this day on we would use our wealth to help the poor. Then, perhaps, when we die we shall be remembered for the little good which we have been able to do.

It is my sincere hope that You will visit us again. You will find our home simpler but, I believe, happier, for we have been changed for the better.

I remain, Your humble and grateful servant,

Dudi Chand

Last Things *Jewish*

'You've been such a good wife to me,' he gasped, and then paused to catch his breath. 'I can't tell you what you mean to me.'

'Shush,' she said, 'not now. You know what the doctor said.' She fluffed up the pillows and straightened the bed-cover. 'There now, lie back and rest.' But there was something he had to say.

'Love of my life, you know everything will be yours after I'm gone.'

She started to cry. 'Don't say such terrible things, dearest. Don't even think about it. The doctor says there's still a good chance. . .'

'We both know there isn't, don't we ?' he protested with all the breath he could summon. 'There's no point hoping against hope. It's better to accept it.' And he fell back on the pillow, staring at the ceiling with his mouth open.

After a while he patted the covers and she came and sat on the bed. Signalling to her to lean over close to him, he whispered, 'Make sure Francesca gets the Porsche.'

'Dearest,' his wife protested. 'You know what a reckless driver she is. Don't you think Marcus should get the Porsche?'

'All right, all right. But let Nigel have the penthouse.'

'But Nigel's got a flat of his own already, and he's hardly ever home anyway. Why don't you let Beatrice have the penthouse?'

'All right, all right. But make sure Abigail and Crispin share the European franchise.'

'Are you crazy? They're for ever arguing with each other. They'd lose the whole deal in no time.'

'Dearest, dearest darling,' he asked her, 'who's dying — you or me?'

The Precious Stone *Hindu*

It was dusk and the air was still, as the wandering holy man settled under a tree, near the big rock, beside the path, at the foot of the mountain. There he would spend the night, with a stone for a pillow. He had few belongings and had long ago given up the idea of becoming successful, or making a lot of money, or even being popular. He had whatever he needed and he needed very little. He had left the world in order to find himself without it.

His evening meditation was disturbed by the shouts of a businessman who came running up to him in an agitated state. 'I'm sure it must be you!' he blurted out. 'I had a dream last night telling me to come to this tree, near the big rock, beside the path, at the foot of the mountain. Here a wandering holy man would give me a priceless stone and I would be rich for ever.

'I've been looking for you all day,' he added in excitement, 'searching, searching, searching. I'm so glad now that I've found you.'

'Perhaps this jewel is the stone from your dream,' said the holy man, rummaging in his bag. 'I happened to see it on the path. Do take it.'

The businessman's mouth dropped open in amazement and his eyes grew large with delight. He had never seen such a huge diamond, had never even dreamed that a diamond could be so enormous. As he carried it away to his home he was glowing with satisfaction and fulfilment. His long day of searching had not been in vain.

But the feeling did not last long and by the end of the evening he was deeply troubled. He tossed and turned all night and couldn't get to sleep. He wanted to plan what he would do with his new riches, and how he would enjoy all his new possessions and wealth, and all the new opportunities life now had in store for him. But he couldn't get the wandering holy man out of his mind, what had happened that day, and what it might all mean.

Before dawn broke he got up and went back to the tree, near the big rock, beside the path, at the foot of the mountain. Disturbing the holy man's morning meditations, he laid the diamond before him. And he asked, 'Please, can I have the precious gift that made you give away this stone?'

That Dying Feeling

She always felt it when leaves began to fall and skies turned grey. Or someone got up to leave. Or something broke. She'd get that dying feeling, a deep sense of loss, a strong fear that time would not wait, that no one would stay for her, that nothing would last, that she herself would not live for ever.

How she dreaded this, how she yearned to hang on. The world was too good, life was too rich, love was too sweet: why must it all end? There must surely be a way to keep it, to go on and on being alive. Surely others had asked these questions? Surely others had found the answers?

'I am old but there is one older than me,' the wise woman of the village explained. 'In the forest far away lives an old man. He, more than anyone, has the secret of living for ever. But if you want to find it, you must travel a long and difficult way, and you must give your whole self to the quest.'

'Old man,' she asked gently when she reached him, 'will you live for ever?"

'I will live,' he sighed, 'until all these trees have fallen to the ground.'

'But one day they will all fall — how can I live for ever?'

'I am old but there is one older than me. By the lake far away lives an old man. He, more than anyone, has the secret of living for ever. But if you want to find it, you must travel a long and difficult way, and you must give your whole self to the quest.'

'Old man,' she asked gently when she reached him, 'will you live for ever?"

'I will live,' he sighed, 'until this lake runs dry.'

'But one day it will run dry — how can I live for ever?'

'I am old but there is one older than me. On the mountain far away lives an old woman. She, more than anyone, has the secret of living for ever. But if you want to find it, you must travel a long and difficult way, and you must give your whole self to the quest.'

'Old woman,' she asked gently when she reached her, 'will you live for ever?"

'I will live,' she sighed, 'until this mountain turns to dust.'

'But surely that will never be,' she thought. 'The mountain will not turn to dust until the sun no longer warms the earth — perhaps now, if I stay with you, I can live for ever!'

The young woman stayed happy on the mountain for hundreds of years. But one day, when the sky was clear and all was still, her home beckoned her, the ones she had loved so far away, the ones whom she had left so long ago.

'You cannot go back!' the old woman warned. 'No one ever should. Nothing stays the same.' But as she spoke she knew that she could not make her stay. 'Take my horse, then, and be back in a day.' Then she held her tightly, her face grew sombre and her voice turned grave: 'For your own sake, no matter what happens, do not get down from the horse.'

She rode like the wind, past the lake and the forest, along the way she had come. But the people she had once known had gone now, and the places were changed for ever. There was nothing — and no one — there for her any more. As light began to fade, she knew she must turn back.

The moon was full and low, and she made good speed till, up ahead, her eyes fell on an overturned cart and the curious sight of hundreds of worn-out shoes, strewn across the road. The horse reared up and then stopped still. Crouched beside the ditch was a wizened figure in a hooded cloak. 'Please help me, dear,' the thin voice wailed. 'The wheel came off my cart, and I am tired and weak.'

She went to move, in order to help. But the old woman's warning flooded back to her: 'For your own sake, no matter what happens, do not get down from the horse.'

'I'd like to help, but I'm sorry . . .'

The poor creature beside the cart creased in pain and let out a plaintive moan. How could she turn her back? How could she just ride on? She got down from the horse and heaved the iron wheel with all her strength. She felt the blood drain from her face, and felt an icy chill run down her back. That dying feeling had returned.

'Thank you, my dear, I hope you won't be sorry!'

'No, that's all right. But tell me: who are you, and what are all these shoes?'

She heard a bitter, hollow laugh, and a firm grip seized her arm. 'I am death, my dear, and these are all the shoes I wore out catching you!'

Out of Fright, out of Mind   muslim

The sea was very choppy that day. But they were all sailors and sons 'of sailors and grandsons. . . and they had seen a lot worse in their time, a lot worse. All except one, that is. Not only had he never been to sea before, he had not even ever paddled on the shore, nor dipped so much as a single toe in the surf.

He felt queasy from the moment they left the harbour and as the boat heaved, he heaved too. But it wasn't until land was out of sight and a terrible storm blew up that he started to panic. 'I want to get off!' he cried.

The others ignored him at first, or told him to pull himself together. One or two of the hands were decent enough to tell him that he'd get his sea legs eventually, and the cabin boy confessed that he had once felt like that, too. But neither their insults nor their comfort made any difference, and he eventually became quite hysterical.

'Can't somebody do something about him?' the captain asked.

'He says he wants to get off,' said the second mate. 'So let's oblige him.' With that, he took hold of the man's legs, the skipper grabbed his arms, and they threw him overboard. The water was cold and rough and dank, and the petrified man was sure he was drowning. He was thrashing around really wildly now, and screaming even louder than before.

They say that in extreme moments, when you suddenly come face to face with death — as in that split second after you have been fatally shot — that your whole life passes before you. Half-conscious now, the man recalled the dearest, the sweetest. . .

In his terror he hadn't noticed that everyone on board had rushed to the side of the deck and were all leaning over. The second mate gave the word, and two of the hands leapt into the water and hauled the man out. He was all right. They wrapped him in blankets, and brought him a hot drink. He calmed down, and was back on his feet in no time.

'That was rather extreme, wasn't it?' the captain said to the second mate. 'But it seems to have done the trick.'

'Yes, you see, cap'n, it wasn't until he was drowning that he realised how safe the ship was. Everything depends on your point of view, I always say, and what you're used to.'

A Handful of Soil

Petros loved the beautiful and holy island of Crete. He had been born there, and had lived all his life there. Now that he was an old man he was ready to leave the earth for heaven, but he did not wish to leave his beloved island, the beautiful and holy island of Crete.

He decided that he would take some of Crete's holy soil to heaven with him. He seized hold of a handful of soil, and kept it firmly gripped in his fist. He sat outside his house, waiting for God to come to collect him, and to take him to heaven.

One day soon God arrived, disguised as a messenger from the king. 'It is time for you to come with me,' said God.

'Yes, I will come,' said Petros.

'But what do you have in your fist?' asked God.

'It is a handful of soil from my beloved and holy island of Crete,' replied Petros, 'I wish to bring it with me.'

'No, you can bring nothing with you,' said God. Petros refused to open his fist and let the soil drop, and God left him. Petros sat for many more years at the door of his house, waiting for God to collect him, and to take him to heaven.

One day after many years God returned, disguised this time as one of Petros's oldest and closest friends. Petros was delighted to see him. 'Come,' said God, 'it is time for you to come with me.'

'Yes, I will come,' said Petros, 'I am ready.'

'But what do you have in your fist?' asked God.

'It is a handful of soil from my beloved and holy island of Crete,' replied Petros, 'I wish to bring it with me.'

'No, you can bring nothing with you,' said God. Petros refused to open his fist and let the soil drop, and God left him. Petros sat for many more years at the door of his house, waiting for God to collect him, and take him to heaven.

One day after many years God returned, disguised this time as Petros's great-grand-daughter. Petros was delighted to see her. 'Come,' she said, 'it is time for you to come with me.' 'Yes, I will come with you,' replied Petros. He looked into her eyes, and he saw there also the eyes of all his other great-grand-children, and he saw the eyes of his grandchildren, and he saw the eyes of his children, and he also saw, as he looked, the eyes of himself when he too had been a tiny trusting child. 'I will come with you,' he said.

'But what do you have in your clenched fist?' she asked. He began to explain, but very gently and sweetly the little child opened his fingers, and he let the soil drop. He went with her to heaven.

And what do you think he saw when he arrived in heaven ? What was the very first thing he saw there?

Yes, there, there in heaven, the first thing he saw was his beloved island, the beautiful and holy island of Crete.

In Search of a Cure

'She's off her rocker! Poor thing — trying to get a cure for her kid: doesn't she know it's dead?'

From house to house she went, from hospital to hospital, from healer to healer. The child lay in her arms, cold and stiff, its eyes staring and vacant. She must get help, she must find wholeness.

Thousands had gathered outside the town to hear the Buddha speak and she edged her way into the crowd. 'Oh High One,' she called, 'please cure my child. I know you can.' The Buddha looked upon her with wisdom and with compassion. 'I have a cure,' he told her, 'but it is not easy to administer. You must knock on every door in the town and bring me some grains of mustard seed from every house where no one has ever died.'

At last someone was taking her seriously, she thought, and she had a real sense of hope. She ran straight down the road in the direction of the town and knocked on the first house she came to. 'Excuse me,' she said when the door was opened. 'I wonder if by chance you could let me have a few grains of mustard seed. I realise this is a funny request coming from a stranger but I would be very grateful. But please forgive me, I must ask you first... has anyone in this household ever died?'

Tears welled up in the householder's eyes. 'Just a few days ago,' he sobbed, 'my wife...'

'Oh dear, I'm so terribly sorry. You must have loved her very much and there must be a great loss in your life. I think I can understand what you've been going through, you see, because...'

And as she started to tell him her story of loving and losing, she saw it reflected in his eyes. He too had loved ... and lost in death ... and their lives were linked.

In every household she visited there was a different tale of grief — a mother, a father, a husband, a wife, a daughter, a son, a brother, a sister, a friend, a colleague. There had been death by fire and by water; by wild beasts and by human hands; by accident and on purpose; through disaster and through disease; slowly and suddenly.

Her heart opened wide as she felt for the first time in her life that all people had suffered — and that they would all die. Her own sorrow seemed different now, for it was somehow part of theirs.

She never did collect mustard seed. She never did go back to the Buddha. He had known all along what she now had discovered for herself.

The Bird, the Forest and the Cage *muslim*

The bird in the cage sang for her owner, a businessman who absolutely adored her. He listened to her sing day and night and served her food and drink in a golden dish. One day he said to her, 'I have to go away on business. What shall I bring you? And when I pass through the forest where you were born, what message shall I give from you to the other birds?'

'Tell them that I am locked in a cage night and day, that I sing only songs yearning for freedom, and that my heart is full of grief. Tell them that I hope that my sorrow will soon end and that we shall fly freely together through the trees. Bring a message from the forest that will put my heart at rest and give me peace of mind. I yearn for my lover, to spread my wings and fly with him across the sky. I shall never be happy until then, for I am cut off from all the good things in life.'

The businessman travelled through the dense forest where he heard the songs of many birds. When he came to a certain spot, he knew at once that he was breathing the very air that his beloved bird had breathed when she had flown there. 'Birds of the forest,' he called. 'Greetings to you from my pretty one! She wants you to know that she is locked in her cage full of sadness and longing, and she asks for a reply which will ease her heart. My love keeps her prisoner behind bars. She wants to join her beloved, sing her songs with a free heart in the open air and fly with him across the skies. But I need her too much — I would miss her song and I cannot let her go.' The birds in the forest listened to these words from the businessman, but none dared speak.

'Aah!' A bird on a branch let out a piercing shriek and fell to the ground. The businessman froze to the spot where he stood and felt the blood drain from his face. A bird suddenly drops dead — whatever can it mean? With a heavy step and a heavy heart he continued on his journey and finally made his way back home.

'What message have you brought me?' the cage-bird asked her owner. Whatever could he say? 'Nothing really. . . there's no message for you,' he said vaguely. 'But what exactly happened? Tell me!' she insisted.

'I don't understand it. I gave them your message as I said I would and suddenly one of them dropped down dead.'

'Aah!' The cage-bird let out a piercing shriek and fell to the floor of her cage. Fear and horror struck the heart of her owner and he cried out in despair, 'Oh what have I done? Now my life means nothing. My moon and sun have fallen from the sky. . . My beloved bird is dead. He opened the door and reached in to take her still, small body in his hand. 'I will bury her now while she is still warm,' he thought. 'Poor dead thing.'

As the businessman lifted the cage-bird out, she swooped up, flew out of the window and perched on a tree nearby. 'Thank you, thank you, thank you for delivering my message. The response of the bird in the forest taught me how to gain true freedom — by dying. When I chose to die, I became free for ever. Now I shall fly to my beloved who is waiting for me. Goodbye, dear man, my master no longer!'

Hanging on for Life   Jewish

'We're damned if we do, Rabbi, and damned if we don't!' I protested. 'There's no way out. If we try to jump over the pit, we'll fall in. If we don't jump, they'll shoot us.'

My words were punctuated by the piercing shriek of the camp guard, imitating once more, and with obvious pleasure, the sound of his machine gun, ' Ra-ta-ta-tat! Ra-ta-ta-tat!' Other guards broke into coarse and callous laughter.

We had been stricken with panic as we were forced, by the brutal butt of a gun, to rush out of our barrack and run here, to this empty space. We'd had some premonition of this earlier in the day when other inmates were made to dig pits in the vacant field. It was an ominous order and we had feared the worst.

'You can choose, you dogs. If you want to live, jump over the pit to the other side. If you don't jump, or if you miss, well... Ra-ta-ta-tat! Ra-ta-ta-tat!' More raucous and ribald jollity.

But what we had not expected — what we hadn't dared imagine — was this sick joke, this particular version of our captors' savagery, their ironic delight in offering us a so-called choice — how liberal of them! They were never short of ideas, and their endless ability to invent new games, their infinite capacity to inflict suffering, never ceased to amaze us.

Pandemonium had broken out in the camp and we could hear behind us the frantic cries of our fellow captives as they, now, were being herded out of the barracks, and a stampede began. In a moment they too would know what fate befell them and they too would have to make the most painful decision of all — how to die.

Ra-ta-ta-tat! Ra-ta-ta-tat!' he went again, exciting our oppressors' malicious mirth.

On either side of me, lined up along the edge of the pit, were living skeletons, exhausted from years of starvation, hard labour, disease and brutal treatment in this pitiless place. We contemplated the abyss before us and the vast expanse of space that stretched through the night to the other side. Below us, clinging to each other in the last moment of life, were the wretched bullet-ridden bodies of those who had tried to jump but failed to reach the other side — and of those who had not tried to jump at all.

'We're damned if we do, Rabbi, and damned if we don't . . .' We had been thrown together so many times, he and I, and there was a special bond between us. Why this should have been — why I, so sceptical about religion, should have found myself drawn to him — I will never know. He represented something I thought I had long ago rejected and yet here, where all the good in the world seemed forsaken, and hope seemed out of reach, his faith and his love never wavered. And they touched something deep within me. 'Let us defy their devilish game,' I suggested, 'Let us die with dignity. Let us simply sit down, you and I, and slide into the pit.'

'Gam zu l'tova!' he answered, his eyes burning with passion. 'This too may be for good! For everything is in the will of God. If it was willed that pits be dug, then pits were dug. And if it was willed that we jump, then we jump. And if we fall, we will reach the world to come . . . So let's jump, and with dignity!'

We held hands and closed our eyes. 'We're jumping,' he whispered deeply.

And when I opened my eyes again, I shuddered. For we were on the other side of the pit. Tears welled up in my eyes and my voice cracked with ecstasy. 'We're alive! We're here! Thank God!' And then, overwhelmed by the mystery, I asked him, 'How did you do it, Rabbi? How did you reach the other side of the pit?'

'I hung on to the faith of our ancestors and the love of our people. I hung on to the memory of my father, and my grandfather, and my great grandfather — may they rest in peace . . . But tell me, how did you do it?'

'Oh Rabbi,' I replied, 'I hung on to you.'

Daring to Fly

Through the gone years, across the now years, in and out the maybe years, it was all the same: her life was relentless, soul-crushing toil.

Washing, scouring, sweeping, scrubbing, patching; hoeing, hacking, digging, pruning, chopping; dragging and pressing; never getting, never reaping; exiled, robbed, emptied, tangled, shackled; never enough knowing, never fully seeing.

This was Miriam's life-world. She had dwelt in it for 16 years, since her birth — though no-one knew for certain where or when she had been born. That was true of all the slaves, they were not allowed to know when exactly and where they had been born. And now Miriam had a baby in the world with her.

Her baby slept on her back as she worked in the plantation, hoeing, chopping, pruning, planting. The sun beat down, the same sun which in Africa had warmed and softened and delighted Miriam's foremothers and forefathers, and all her other ancestors, but which now, in the slavery-land of America, was hard and ferocious; cruel, pitiless and implacable; savage in its casual, unthinking, careless brutality.

Tiny babies do not slumber long, least of all when they are empty and thirsting, and when their mothers are stretched with pain and worry. Miriam's baby awoke on her back, and began to cry. He cried out at the sun, at the plantation, at his whole life-world. He cried for softness, for tender love spa-

ciously given. 'Stop that!. Strangle that thing's noise!. Stop it, put an end to it, I say!' The plantation overseer rode up to Miriam, cracking his whip. She looked up wearily at his white face, towering on his horse high above her, and her baby son continued to cry.

Crack, the overseer lashed both Miriam and her baby deep into their skin. She fell sobbing to her knees as her baby screamed, and the overseer rode on, forgetting Miriam and her life-world in less time than it takes to crack a whip.

An old slave, Moses, happened to see. He came over to Miriam. 'You must go, little mother, it is time for you to go. You can dare to fly, you know, daughter, you can dare fly to Africa. Kum yali, kum buba tambe, fly, little sister, fly. You shall be the first, you shall be the mother of us all.'

She stepped up on to the air. First with one foot, then with the other. Next she was gliding, and her whip wound was healed, and her baby's wound was healed, and she was floating, soaring into the breeze, free as an eagle, and she was on her way now, on her way home. The overseer on the land beneath her caught sight of her, and he roared with fury, and he began to pursue her. But on she flew, over the fields, over the fences, over the cabins, over the streams, over the woods, and out of sight.

The next day four young male slaves dropped exhausted where they were working, and were lashed without mercy by the overseer, and left for dead. ' Kum yali, kum buba tambe,' whispered Moses approaching them. 'Dare to fly, my young brothers, fly away home, fly to your Africa.'

The overseer boiled with fury as he saw the four young men, beautiful now, stepping up on to the air, first with one foot and then with the other, and floating and gliding over the fields, over the fences, over the cabins, over the streams, over the woods, and out of sight. He hurried away to report the matter to the slave-owner.

'It's time for us all to go,' murmured Moses. ' Kum yali, kum buba tambe. All of us must dare.' And he moved swiftly through the plantation, partly running and partly flying, speaking to everyone. And each and every slave, every woman and every man, every girl and every boy, stepped up on the air, first with one foot and then with the other, and they all hovered in the air above the slave-owner and the overseer on their horses, and then they turned and rose higher, like eagles, free in the bright air.

Soaring, rising, floating, gliding; hoping, willing, dreaming, trusting; cherishing, dancing, singing, praising; pulsing with beauty, rejoicing in their own strength and grace; firm and determined, with their love into freedom; and on their way home now, to give birth to new life.

The story soon began to spread around, about how the people dared fly. Oh they tried to suppress it, the slave-owners, but there was no way now the story could be suppressed. All over slavery-land the story was told, and year after year. Even after the slavery-time, people still told the story.

And even outside of slavery-land the story is known.

In prisons and war zones everywhere, on treadmills and conveyor belts in all lands, in homes and workplaces, markets and arenas, parks and fields, in Africa, Europe, Asia, the Americas, in our hearts and in our memories, we cherish that special day, and those special words, 'kum yali, kum buba tambe', and we cherish that it has happened, and that it has been learned, that people dare fly.

Whoever Comes This Way

Strange how the grass never grows over that spot. All around the grass is luscious in the rainy season, wispy in the drought. But there, just there, not a thing takes root. As if they'd learned the secret of the spot, no animals dare cross it. And travellers passing by stop in their tracks and step aside, as if gripped by an ancient taboo.

They say it's where a tortoise met her death. Plodding along, she heard a lion roar and saw it bound towards her from the jungle... She pulled her head inside her shell — and felt the creature pounce. Claws drawn, he rolled her over and she lay gasping on her back. And that was that, she knew: the hunt was up.

'Wait, please,' she cried. 'If I fight you, you will win. For you are big and I am small. You are strong and I am weak. You are fast and I am slow. But I have something else. Grant me this, I beg, one last request: a moment for myself before I die. Then you will surely have me for your prey.'

The lion loosed his grip and stood aside. It cost him nothing: he would take her soon. She leapt upon her feet and scratched the ground, pulling the grass out by its very roots. She kicked and scraped and dug and tore and raked. She saw the mound of earth she'd made and then she stopped.

'You are big and I am small. You are strong and I am weak. You are fast and I am slow. But I have something else. Whoever comes this way will see and know: I struggled to the end.'

5
Listening with your Eyes

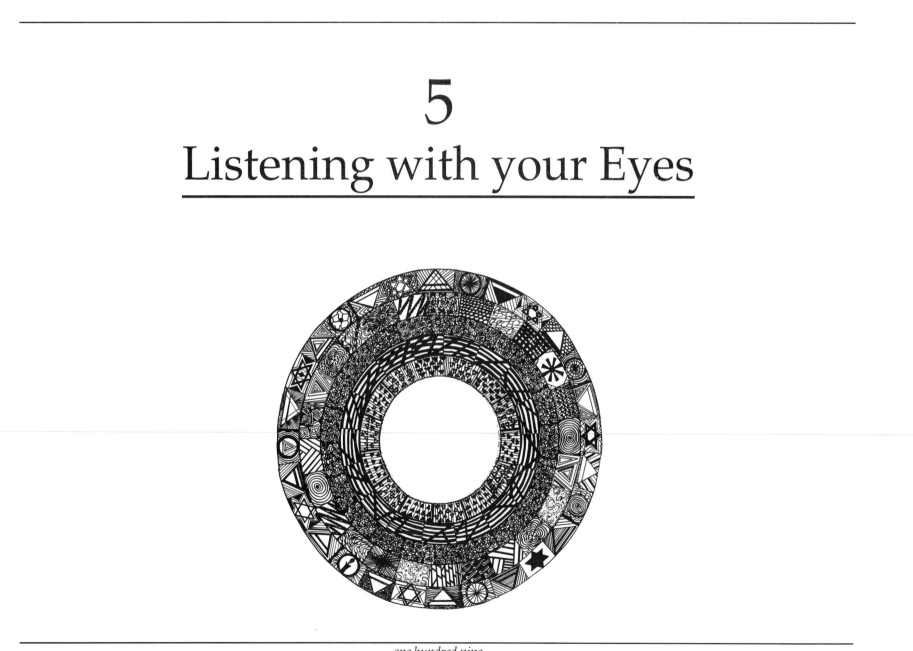

Contents of this chapter

Listening with your Eyes . . . and Are You Sitting Comfortably?

'Listen, children, listen with your eyes and with your nose.' It is with some such words as these that traditional storytellers, all over the world, begin their tales.

For a crucial aspect of the storyteller's craft is helping your listeners to pay close attention: helping them to hang on to every word and phrase you use, to follow the story with intense concentration through its every twist and turn, and to see the events, encounters and settings in vivid outline and colour in their mind's eye. It is only if you can get people to attend single-mindedly to the outer surface of a story that you can reasonably hope that they will grasp, or be grasped by, its deeper and inner meaning.

Attentiveness depends on comfort, both literally and metaphorically: listeners need to be feeling comfortable not only physically but also psychologically, with a sense of security and contentment, feeling at peace and at ease. So another traditional way of starting a story, besides 'Listen with your eyes. . .', is always 'Are you sitting comfortably?'

Both attentiveness and comfort are particularly important with stories which have an inner or deeper meaning, and which require listeners to be patient and persistent if the meaning is to be discovered. Yet in many school classrooms, perhaps particularly in secondary schools, you cannot rely on attentiveness and comfort being automatically present — there are so many distractions and unpredictable happenings, and the pupils are more likely than not to have a myriad of things on their minds totally unconnected with the subject-matter you wish to present to them.

For these reasons it's often valuable to use various kinds of simple activity or exercise in order to get pupils to pay close attention and to feel comfortable, and in order to explore a story's possible meanings without being inappropriately or prematurely intellectual and cerebral. So here, in this section of this book, are reminders about simple exercises or activities which can be used with almost any story. Of course, not all the activities described here are equally usable in every possible educational setting. But all, in principle, can promote the two basic circumstances which are necessary if the inner meaning of a story is to stand a chance of being grasped: attentiveness on the one hand and comfort on the other.

Each activity is outlined under the same three headings:

What:
A description in a nutshell of what the activity entails.

How:
Indications about classroom organisation, and any necessary preparation.

Why:
Brief listing of the benefits for pupils.

When an exercise has been completed, there may be no need for any further work or discussion. Often, however, an exercise can be a useful preliminary to conventional discussion or writing about a story's meanings.

1) Sequencing

What:

❂ Cutting up a text and getting pupils to piece it together again.

How:

❂ Preferable to divide class into small groups — each member of a group holds one of the pieces of the text and reads it aloud to other members;

❂ Possible also to work with the whole class — have text on large pieces of poster paper round room, or on overhead projector.

Why:

❂ If carried out in small groups, pupils listen to each other closely, collaborate on the task, respecting each other and develop self-respect, because everyone holds an indispensable resource!

❂ Pupils attend to issues of causality and consequence, and therefore develop skills of speculation, reasoning and justifying.

❂ Pupils become aware of the range of techniques which storytellers use to signal cause and effect, pace and sequence.

❂ Pupils develop self-confidence, through having a sense of being in charge of the material.

2) Interrupting

What:

❂ Breaking into the telling or reading of a story with a question or query.

How:

❂ Can be a whole class or small group activity, led by either the teacher or pupils.

❂ Questions to answer or to ponder include the following:

❂ What do you think is going to happen next? — give as many ideas as you can within the space of two minutes.

❂ What do you think a particular character may be thinking or feeling just at the moment?

❂ If you could enter the story at this stage and speak to the characters, what would you ask or say?

❂ Make up some additional information about one of the characters — what they look like, what their private interests and hobbies are, what they had for breakfast this morning, what makes them laugh.

❂ Imagine the scene vividly in your mind's eye. What can you see? Describe the colours, the movements, the view. And what can you hear? What can you smell and touch?

Why:

❂ Pupils enter more fully with their imagination into the story's events, and become more interested to know what is going to happen.

❂ Pupils have to fantasise, guess and speculate, and to develop certain storytelling skills themselves.

3) Factual Quizzes

What:

✪ Giving a test or quiz about factual details in a story which has been told or read.

How:

✪ The teacher prepares a set of questions in advance, and presents these to the pupils either before or after the story is told or read.

✪ The pupils themselves can construct a quiz after they have heard the story, everyone trying to ask as difficult a question as possible.

✪ It may be useful to tell or read a story twice, with the second presentation coming after the quiz, and thus enabling pupils to 'correct' their previous answers, or to fill in gaps.

Why:

✪ Pupils have to listen particularly carefully.

✪ Pupils derive enjoyment and satisfaction from memorising small details, and from answering questions correctly.

✪ Pupils are helped to distinguish between details which are essential and details which are irrelevant to the story's meaning, and to note that part of a storyteller's craft is to include irrelevant details for the sake of maintaining interest and giving a sense of reality.

4) Frozen Frames

What:

✪ Asking pupils to imagine and represent a single scene from a story, in order to illustrate the story as a whole.

How:

✪ In small groups or as individuals pupils can describe their chosen scene in words, or else sketch it with a rough drawing.

✪ In small groups, pupils can 'sculpt' their chosen scene, by creating a tableau; it may be valuable to sketch or photograph the tableaux which are presented, in order to promote and focus further discussion. These might be used to create a photo album depicting stages in the life of a character in the story; alternatively, one picture might be chosen for the 'book cover' of the story.

Why:

✪ Pupils have to choose and respond to what they feel is a particularly significant episode in a story.

✪ Pupils may well discover, intuitively through processes of visualising and sculpting, a story's deeper meanings — or may legitimately add to a story's deeper meanings.

✪ Pupils may discover ways of adapting or developing a story.

✪ Pupils are helped to remember a story in its entirety by having to focus in great detail on just one particular scene or episode.

5) **Interrogating**

What:

✪ Getting pupils to ask masses of questions about a story or part of a story.

How:

✪ If working as individuals, each pupil has a piece of text printed on a largish sheet of paper with plenty of space in the two margins, 'and above and beneath.

✪ If working in small groups, each group has a very large sheet, with a story or extract from a story glued in the middle.

✪ In the margins round the text pupils write brief questions. Some of the questions can be factual (what colour hair does this person have?), and others can be entirely speculative (what did she dream about last night?). The important thing is to write down as many questions as possible.

✪ Once lots of questions have been asked, pupils speculate about some of the possible answers, and choose which questions seem most relevant to understanding the story's meaning.

Why:

✪ Pupils have to be imaginative, and therefore become more receptive to a story's meanings.

✪ Pupils are required to pay closer attention than might otherwise be the case.

✪ Pupils become aware of the techniques and skills used by the storyteller.

✪ Pupils derive self-confidence from feeling that they are in charge of the material which is being presented to them, rather than being merely passive recipients or consumers.

6) **Cloze Procedure**

What:

✪ Blotting out certain words in a piece of text, and getting pupils to decide how the gaps thus created ought to be filled in.

How:

✪ Either you blot out certain particularly significant words, essential for understanding a story's meaning, or else you blot out — for example — every seventh word, regardless of how important it may happen to be.

✪ The story with its gaps can be presented to the whole class through being read aloud, or else in writing on a blackboard, flipchart or overhead projector; or can be given to the 'leader' of a small group who reads it slowly to the rest of the group; or can be worked on by each individual pupil, followed by class or small group discussion, comparing and contrasting the various suggestions which are made.

✪ Whichever method one uses, it is important to get pupils to think of at least two separate possibilities for each gap, so that they have to reason and to choose.

Why:

✪ Pupils have to attend closely to the sequence of events in a story, and to points of style and register in the storyteller's language.

✪ Pupils have to draw on the full range of their own linguistic resources, and may well extend their active or passive vocabulary.

✪ Pupils develop self-confidence from knowing that there is seldom a single 'correct' answer, and from seeing that their own suggestions are sometimes preferable to the words used by the original storyteller.

✪ Pupils find the exercise both simple and challenging, and therefore also enjoyable and satisfying.

7) Messages

What:

☯ Getting pupils to summarise a story's point or message with a slogan, phrase or proverbial saying.

How:

☯ You can prepare in advance a set of phrases of the kinds which appear on lapel badges or on greetings cards, or prepare a set of proverbs. Pupils choose from these, or adapt them, or use them as models for writing their own.

☯ Instead, you can get the pupils to work 'from cold', inventing their own ideas and suggestions

☯ Either way, the task is for pupils to summarise what they take to be a story's message or moral, and to do this in a pithy and striking way.

☯ It's useful to distinguish between two main types of summarising phrase, and to get pupils to consider both: (a) phrases which only make sense to people who know the story, and (b) phrases whose meaning is clear regardless of whether or not the story is known.

☯ It's important that pupils should compare and contrast different suggestions for summarising the same story, and should have to choose between alternatives, giving their reasons.

Why:

☯ Pupils are helped to explore and articulate a story's basic meaning.

☯ By having a brief summary in the form of a pithy phrase or saying pupils are helped to remember the story.

☯ Pupils use and develop their imagination and their ability to express complex ideas through metaphor and allusion.

8) Beginnings

What:

☯ Giving pupils examples of the many different ways in which a story can begin.

How:

☯ The teacher reads slowly the first sentence of between 6 and 9 different stories, and gives a key word for each to help pupils remember them.

☯ Instead, between 6 and 9 sentences are provided to pupils in writing. They can be on large sheets of paper round the walls of the classroom, or else of course each pupil can have their own set. If pupils work in small groups then each group can have a set of the sentences, and it may well be valuable then for each sentence to be provided on its own separate piece of paper.

☯ Either way, the basic activity is to compare and contrast, and to sort and rank. Pupils can be asked to do tasks such as the following:

☯ Rank these sentences in order of interest.

☯ Choose the 3 which strike you as most traditional.

☯ Choose the 3 which strike you as most unusual.

☯ Describe 3 different techniques which storytellers use to gain interest.

☯ For any 3 of the sentences name one advantage and one disadvantage.

Why:

☯ Pupils are likely to be keen to hear the stories whose first sentences have attracted their initial interest.

☯ Pupils are helped to recognise and appreciate standard narrative techniques, and can be encouraged to use some of these in stories which they themselves write.

9) Memory Experiments

What:

✿ Conducting experiments to find out which parts of a story most easily get lost in the telling, and under what circumstances.

How:

✿ One common and enjoyable exercise involves a story being passed along a chain. About 6 pupils leave the classroom, and then come back in one at a time. A story is read to the first, who re-tells it to the second, who re-tells it to the third, and so on, with the rest of the class watching and listening, and perhaps making notes.

✿ Another possibility is to tell the same story in different ways to different audiences (either small groups or else individual pupils), and to note the differences between the ways in which the story is retained and understood. The range of different styles includes:

✿ The teller and the listeners sitting with their backs to each other, so that there is no eye contact or mutual awareness of facial expression.

✿ The teller and listeners face to face, so that they can see each other's responses.

✿ Again face to face, but this time with the teller using gesture, actions, different voices and accents for different characters, repetition, ad libs, topical and local references, and so on.

Why:

✿ Pupils are likely to find the exercise very enjoyable, and to be interested in watching how their memory, and the memory of others, works.

✿ Pupils become aware of the most salient features of the story under consideration.

✿ Pupils learn to distinguish between essential and non-essential details in a story, but appreciate also that a certain amount of 'padding' is an important part of most storytelling.

✿ Pupils appreciate certain important storytelling techniques, for example the use of repetition, alliteration, cadence, unusual tiny details, pattern, strong visual images, expressive and evocative language, and so on.

10) Exploring with Pictures

What:

✪ Getting pupils to explore their responses to a story by choosing or making pictures.

How:

✪ There is a large display of photographs on the walls of the classroom, or on some of the furniture. Alternatively, each small group of pupils can be given a pack of — for example — black and white postcard-size photographs.

✪ A story is read or told to the class as a whole.

✪ First as individuals, but subsequently in pairs or small groups, pupils choose from the display the image, or the pair of images, which best expresses for them what the story they have just heard was really about.

✪ Instead, pupils can be given piles of old magazines, and be asked to create collages which illustrate what they felt the story was about.

Why:

✪ Pupils are likely to find it much easier, in the first instance, to respond to a story non-verbally and non-cerebrally rather than through intellectual discussion.

✪ Pupils are reminded that photographs and collages, like stories, involve selection, framing, perspective, juxtaposition, composition, and so on.

11) Re-telling and re-writing

What:

✪ Getting pupils to re-tell or re-write a story from a different point of view, in a different style, or in a different context.

How:

✪ The possibilities include:

✪ Tell the story from the point of view of one of the characters, including reference to feelings and perceptions not mentioned in the original, and to events which are no more than touched on or alluded to.

✪ Tell the story or part of the story in verse; or as an article in a tabloid newspaper; or as a television script; or as a telegram; or (assuming it is not already written in heightened language) in a poetic, epic style.

✪ Transpose the story to a different culture, and to a different period of history.

Why:

✪ Pupils have to identify and attend to the most important features in a story.

✪ Pupils may well develop new meanings, and in this way they are engaging in a living process of passing traditional stories on from one age to another, and from one culture to another.

✪ Pupils practise certain skills of storytelling, and may develop these further by comparing and contrasting their own efforts with those of others.

12) **Realia**

What:

✪ Getting pupils to imagine and write small scraps of material to fill in a story's background.

How:

✪ The possibilities include: a shopping list; letters and notes of various kinds, both formal and informal; notices; advertisements; news cuttings; extracts from a school report or record of achievement; drafts and jottings; diary extracts; a telegram; publicity leaflets; greetings cards; telephone messages.

✪ A collection of realia can then be used to make a scrapbook or wall display.

Why:

✪ Pupils are encouraged to use wit, humour and imagination.

✪ Pupils are helped to remember the main outline of a story.

✪ Pupils may discover additional meanings for the story, or invent new details.

13) **Guided Fantasy**

What:

✪ Getting the pupils to visualise the scenes and events in a story as vividly as possible in their mind's eye.

How:

✪ Pupils close their eyes. A story is read to them quite slowly, with frequent pauses, and it may be important to add questions and instructions. ('What is the colour of her dress?' 'What is the quality of the light?' 'What can you see in the distance?'). They concentrate as fully as possible, and try to visualise all the events and scenes.

✪ It may well be useful to preface the reading with a relaxation exercise, so that pupils start by attending closely to their own sensations and feelings before they try attending to the story. Also a relaxation exercise will help them to still their minds, and this will in turn make it easier for them to concentrate on the story.

✪ Instead or as well, by way of preparation, it may be valuable to get pupils to concentrate very attentively on certain objects in the classroom.

✪ At the end of the guided fantasy, it is important to bring pupils back to the present very gently, and to give them plenty of space to describe and reflect on what they 'saw'.

Why

✪ Pupils use and develop their imaginations and capacities for empathy.

✪ Pupils are likely to remember the story far more vividly.

✪ Pupils are likely to invent new details and events, and to find that the story takes on a new life of its own.

14) **Keywords**

What:

❂ Getting pupils to join in the recitation of an important brief passage from a story.

How:

❂ The teacher chooses a briefish passage (say, around 50 to 70 words at most, and quite possibly much less) from a particular story. The passage should preferably be in epic or poetic language, and should be a significant part of the story under consideration

❂ The passage is read slowly to the class four times, as follows:

1 An ordinary straightforward reading, with everyone listening as carefully as possible.

2 Pupils this time listen for what they consider to be certain keywords, and each pupil chooses between 3 and 5.

3 Pupils say aloud the keywords which they have chosen, when they are spoken by the reader.

4 Each pupil tries to join in reciting the passage as fully as possible, speaking along with the reader.

Why

❂ Pupils use and develop their listening skills.

❂ Pupils note and appreciate heightened language and the use of metaphor and cadence.

❂ Pupils are reminded by the choral aspect of the fourth reading that storytelling is at best a kind of performance, and that it involves the use of ritual and repetition.

15) **Working with Quotations**

What:

❂ Getting pupils to reflect on the nature and purpose of storytelling and storylistening.

How:

❂ Working in pairs or small groups, pupils read, discuss, select and rank a set of quotations, such as those given on pages 120-121.

❂ The quotations may be ranked according to the interest they have for the pupils or the importance they attach to them. Alternatively, pupils may be asked to select quotations which are very similar to — or different from — each other in meaning.

❂ This will probably be most effective when the pupils have had opportunities to read and consider a range of stories and are likely to have internalised a concept of 'story' as such.

Why:

❂Pupils develop a theoretical understanding of the role of story in human cultures and its value for individuals.

The Nature of Story: some readings on the theme

■ **Inside every single story**

'But why do you hate stories so much?' Haroun blurted, feeling stunned. 'Stories are fun . . .'

'The world, however, is not for Fun,' Khattam-Shud replied. 'The world is for Controlling.'

'Which world?' Haroun made himself ask.

'Your world, my world, all worlds,' came the reply. 'They are all there to be Ruled. And inside every single story, inside every stream in the Ocean, there lies a world, a story-world, that I cannot Rule at all. And that is the reason why.'

Salman Rushdie, *Haroun and the Sea of Stories*, 1990

■ **Cunning and high spirits**

'Fairy tales taught humankind in the past, and continue to teach children in the present, that the way to meet dark mythical forces is with cunning and high spirits.'

Walter Benjamin, *The Storyteller*

■ **Mend and restore**

'The Baal Shem Tov, when he saw the lines of communication with heaven were broken and it was impossible to mend them with prayer ... used to mend them and restore them by telling a tale.'

Rabbi Nachman of Bratslav, quoted by Yaffa Eliach in *Hasidic Tales of the Holocaust*, 1982

■ **Source of enchantment**

'Looking at them from outside, one may think that the people in an Indian village community lack the amenities of modern life; but actually they have no sense of missing much; on the contrary, they give an impression of living in a continual state of secret enchantment. The source of enchantment is the storyteller in their midst...'

R.K.Narayan, *The World of the Storyteller*, 1987

■ **Born again**

Each time a story is told, it is born again for the listener and for the storyteller.

Bob Barton, *Tell Me Another*, 1987.

■ The way and the lifestyle

'Jesus' biggest and most innovative decision was the manner in which he chose to preach. He chose the way and the lifestyle of the storyteller, the parable-maker who fashions a new creation out of the holy materials of the only creation we all share in common : the birds, the lilies of the field, the fishes caught, the fig tree in bloom, the sheep versus the goats, the leaven in the bread.'

Matthew Fox, *Original Blessing*, 1983.

■ Some day you will be old enough

'My Dear Lucy, I wrote this story for you, but when I began it I had not realised that girls grow quicker than books. As a result you are already too old for fairy tales, and by the time it is printed and bound you will be older still. But some day you will be old enough to start reading fairy tales again...'

C.S.Lewis, at the start of *The Lion The Witch and The Wardrobe*, 1950.

■ That sort of bear

'What about a story?' said Christopher Robin.

'What about a story?' I said.

'Could you very sweetly tell Winnie-the-Pooh one?'

'I suppose I could,' I said. 'What sort of stories does he like?'

'About himself. Because he's that sort of bear.'

A.A. Milne, *Winnie the Pooh*

■ More than food

'Remember only this one thing,' said Badger. 'The stories people tell have a way of taking care of them. If stories come to you, care for them. And learn to give them away where they are needed. Sometimes a person needs a story more than food to stay alive; that is why we put these stories in each other's memory. This is how people care for themselves.'

Barry Lopez, *Crow and Weasel*, 1990.

■ Appetite for life

What stories ultimately satisfy is life's hunger for itself, its desire to exist, its desire to be turned on, its desire to be given form and made able to flow. We consume stories most eagerly in infancy and then again in our adolescence, at just the times, that is, when our appetite for life is at its strongest. We want to join the game, and stories form and equip us to do so.

Don Cupitt, *What is a Story?*, 1991

6
Once Upon a Time

Once Upon a Time . . . and So the Story Goes —
origins, backgrounds, treatments, reflections

Introductory notes

All the stories in this book are original with regard to their phrasings, syntax and detail. All, however, are derived from oral traditions, and most exist in writing in other versions elsewhere. Some of the renderings are entirely faithful to the tradition, but others have been given fresh emphases and references. In addition, several have been transposed from pre-industrial to modern cultural contexts, and these are presented in a variety of modern genres.

In the notes which follow, there is information about each story with regard to its origin and background, and there are some comments on the way it has been treated. Teachers may wish to know and to mention these points when they are handling a story with pupils in the classroom.

Further, there are reflections on some of the main questions which each story raises, invites and explores, and which teachers may wish to use when leading and focusing discussions. These reflections are for teachers' own private consideration in the first instance, not for putting directly to pupils.

First, in the notes which follow, there is reference to the ten *Story Stories*, lettered A- J, which appear on pages 9-20. Then, numbered 1-50, there is reference to the stories which appear in the section entitled *From Tadpole to Butterfly.*

STORY STORIES

☐ A What Sort of a Person? (page 9)

Origin
Modern.

Background
The story has a variety of versions, according to the teller's immediate purpose. It is usually told in order to poke fun at the person on the ground. (In one current version, for example, the person on the ground is an inspector of schools! Other versions make him or her a headteacher, a politician, a bishop, or a popstar.)

Treatment
Conventional, but the joke element in other versions has been converted here to make a philosophical point about the nature of stories.

Reflection
How do these three people happen to be together? What have they been talking to each other about before the story begins? What is being said at the end about the nature of stories? In what ways does this story itself have the features of story to which the child refers? Why is it the child, and not either of the others, who can guess something about the real nature of the person on the ground?

☐ B Because of the Seed (page 10)

Origin
Iraq, Muslim tradition.

Background
A sultan was the leader of a Muslim community in countries of the Middle East, and was expected to rule and govern with wisdom, compassion and justice. The claim made by this story, that traditional stories stimulate and nourish qualities of wisdom and justice, is to be found in a wide range of world cultures.

Treatment
The traditional tale is re-told, but with additional emphasis on the nature of story and narrative.

Reflection
What are the stories that I was told when I was very little? In what ways may these have contained seeds which made me kind and strong? Did my storytellers ensure that I was sitting comfortably? How important was this? Why do small children love stories? Is this a 'true' story? How could I find out?

☐ C Forest, Fire and Prayer (page 11)

Origin
Jewish, East European Hasidic.

Background
The four rabbis mentioned here were all great leaders in the history of East European Judaism. Rabbi Baal Shem Tov (1700 -1760), the first of the rabbis in this story, is the most famous and influential figure of Hasidic Judaism, a movement whose purpose was to renew traditions of prayer and spirituality, and teachings about the importance of humanitarian service. It expressed and shared its insights particularly through stories.

Treatment
Conventional narrative style. The story has been constructed so that it can be used for a sequencing exercise (see page 112).

Reflection
Why was it important to go to the right place in the forest? Why was lighting a fire important? Why, eventually, did only the story matter? Who wrote down this story, and why? Is it really more important to tell stories than to say prayers, and if so why? Does God prefer stories to prayers and ritual actions and, if so, why might this be?

☐ D Nights and Mornings (page 12)

Origin
Middle East, within Islamic traditions.

Background
This is the core story at the heart of the collection known as *The Arabian Nights*, one of the most famous and influential collections of oral tradition in the whole history of humankind. Another rendering of the main character's name is of course Scheherazade. The collection contains versions of many of the world's best known tales, including those of *Aladdin* and *Sinbad*.

Treatment
The traditional tale is re-told, but with emphasis on the ways in which the 1001 stories kindle mutual affection and love between Shahrazad and the king, and on the context of Islamic culture and devotional belief in which the original stories were collected and transmitted.

Reflection
What is the connection between depression and cruelty? What is the power that Shahrazad holds over the king? How is it different from the power which he holds over others? What does he find attractive in her? And she in him? Can I think of any times in my own life when stories have helped to stop me from being depressed? And when have they caused me to like or to love someone else? What do I learn from this story about Islamic beliefs in the compassion and love of God?

☐ E Your Own Story (page 14)

Origin
Christian, and versions exist also in other traditions about the sayings of religious teachers.

Background
There is a strand in all religious traditions which stresses the importance of each individual person seeing their life as a story, with a purpose and pattern, and of seeing that religion is part of this story. Stories in scriptures and sacred writings, according to this view, remain lifeless and irrelevant unless and until they cast light on the personal life-stories of individuals.

Treatment
The story is told here in the traditional form of 'a saying of the guru' — that is, the recollection of a brief conversational exchange between a teacher and a disciple.

Reflection
Has the disciple ever read a good book? Does the goodness of a good book lie its content or in the way you read it? What experiences has the teacher had to enable this reply to the disciple to be given? What will the disciple do next?

☐ F Put to the Test (page 15)

Origin
Sufi tradition within Islam.

Background
The Sufi tradition lays emphasis on stories and symbols as ways of expressing and communicating religious insights, and frequently makes use of paradox to show that religious truth cannot be expressed directly. A recurring concern, as here, is to show that mature religious faith is different from believing various improbable or impossible fantasies.

Treatment
The original story is modernised by being told in the first person, and through some of the references.

Reflection
Why should anyone want to be 'holy'? What use or value is it? Is the desire to be holy a holy desire? What does the narrator see in the king that the king cannot see for himself? What is the difference between the various kinds of thing the king is asked to believe? Is he wiser at the end? What might he be up to next?

☐ G Naked Truth (page 16)

Origin
Modern secular.

Background
The idea of truth being 'clothed' in imagery, metaphor or story is found in a wide range of world cultures.

Treatment
The original story is told here in modern mid-American slang, in order to give a sense that its basic theme is of contemporary relevance.

Reflection
Is truth ever 'naked' — or do we see and speak truth only in stories and images? What are the features of well-dressed truth? How important is it for truth to be dressed in the latest fashion? What are the dangers of it trying to be fashionable? Can truth stand outside fashion altogether?

☐ H The Book (page 17)

Origin
Christian, from the desert mystics of the early church.

Background
The desert mystics or 'fathers' used paradoxes, riddles and puzzles such as this as an aid to meditation on the infinite and wordless nature of God, and in order to encapsulate their insights and teachings.

Treatment
The traditional story is told here in the form of a brief exchange of conversation.

Reflection
Who are the two people here, and what is the relationship between them? What will be the next remark, comment or question in this exchange? Is Serapion wise or foolish? What will happen to him? How will they cope now that they no longer have a book? Will it be harder or easier to carry on caring about the poor?

☐ I Seed Progress Report (page 18)

Origin

Christian — the parable of the sower in Matthew 13 : 3-8, Mark 4 : 1-9, and Luke 8 : 4-8.

Background

The original parable — 'a sower went forth to sow' — describes four different kinds of response to the gospel ('the good news', 'the word') preached by Jesus. It is in particular in Matthew's story (verses 18-23) that the parable is interpreted, and in which Jesus explains why he presents and shares his message to humankind through parables and stories. By extension, the parable is perhaps about the differential responses which may be made to any story.

Treatment

The four different responses to preaching and to story are presented here in a modern setting, in the context of a report to shareholders about a marketing campaign for a desktop publishing package. There are references to seeds, growth and transformation, reminiscent of aspects of the original parable.

Reflection

If I were to visit these four places — Appatheaton, Brashbury, Cooloffham and Deapchangeley — what differences between them might I find as I walked down their respective high streets? If I were to stay for a week in each of these four towns, what are the different ways in which I might be treated by the inhabitants? What do I suspect are Deapchangeley's secrets? What concrete examples might I find in Deapchangeley of sensitivity, enlightenment, empowerment, delight?

☐ J The Real Thing (page 20)

Origin

Modern secular.

Background

The difference between writing to someone and speaking to them face-to-face is a common experience in a very wide range of relationships, and provides a useful metaphor for the difference between merely reading a text (for example, a story) on the one hand and actually understanding it on the other.

Treatment

The theme is presented through the context of a relationship between a woman and a man.

Reflection

Why doesn't he actually speak to her? Why doesn't he send the letters? Is it that he doesn't really love her? Does he know what love is? Does she? Why does she take the initiative, and arrange to see him? Why does she lean forward to kiss him? What will happen next? Any chance that they will live happily ever after?

FROM TADPOLE TO BUTTERFLY

☐ **1 Thrown to the World (page 38)**

Origin

Modern, but using traditional motifs and symbols, and a traditional narrative style.

Background

It is sometimes suggested that refugees, asylum-seekers and migrants are representative human beings, and that their plight and situation reflect and cast light on the needs and priorities of all.

Treatment

The story recalls the traditional fairy-tale motif of godparents bringing gifts and wishes for a newborn baby. The names and historical circumstances of the characters are left unstated, in order to emphasise their representative or symbolic nature.

Reflection

Would the gifts and blessings be different if the family were not refugees? What gifts and blessings would I myself have liked to receive at birth? Which would I give to a child of my own? Do I have, amongst my own possessions, a stone, a bracelet, a prayer-book, a compass, a ring, a flower in bud? Am I, have I ever been, a refugee? Which stories in this book best illustrate the grandmother's remarks about the subject matter of stories?

☐ **2 Born from the Waves (page 40)**

Origin

New Zealand, a Maori myth.

Background

Maui is a mischievous god in Maori mythology, who is frequently depicted playing tricks.

Treatment

The story is told here in a traditional epic style.

Reflection

How is it that Maui survived his time in the sea? Did his mother really think that he would drown, or was she testing his strength? Why did he feel later that he needed to see and touch his mother? In what way is each of us 'born from the waves'? Do we all need to search for our own home?

☐ 3   Hush My Baby (page 42)

Origin
Jewish.

Background
The story contains a *midrash* — a traditional Jewish story whose purpose is to explain or explore the reasons why something exists, or how a situation has come about.

Treatment
The original rabbinic version is placed within the account of a day in the working life of a paediatrician.

Reflection
What is the full range of anxieties which the mothers express or imply? What is the difference between the last answer which the doctor gives and all the others? How do I explain this? What is likely to be the impact on the mother?

☐ 4   In the Dark and the Day (page 43)

Origin
Modern.

Background
The imagery of night and day is found in all oral traditions of storytelling.

Treatment
Conventional narrative style, with no details about the names and circumstances of the characters.

Reflection
Were there really ghosts in the garden? Did the charm really make them go away? Or was the father deceiving the child? If so, which deception was more serious — to tell her that there were ghosts, or to tell her that the charm was effective? Do adults sometimes practise other deceptions such as these? What is the story saying about growing up?

☐ 5 I Don't Know What To Do (page 44)

Origin
Traditional folktale from Kerala, South India.

Background
In all cultures there are exaggerated and improbable stories about dilemmas which people may encounter in their everyday lives, and which are told and discussed in order to explore real moral issues.

Treatment
The original dilemma is retained, but the setting is transposed to a radio phone-in programme.

Reflection
What does the agony expert do to try to inspire the caller's confidence? If the conversation continued, what could the expert do to help the caller make up her own mind what to do? What could the expert advise the caller to do? Which would the caller prefer — to be told what to do, or to make up her own mind? What, in any case, is the real dilemma? Have I ever encountered a dilemma which, deep down, was like this? What guidance, if any, did I get from others?

☐ 6 Look Up, Children (page 46)

Origin
Native American.

Background
Many legends are about leaders and heroes whose victories were over external forces. This story, however, celebrates creativity — including art and storytelling — in the life of the individual and the community.

Treatment
The original story is framed here by a modern context, in order to enhance its relevance and power as an explanatory tool.

Reflection
Why do the children wish to hear the story yet again? What touches their own experience of life? Why did the boy want to be like the others? What did they represent for his people? Was the boy's mother right to tell him not to expect to be like other boys? How can we respond to, or explain, the boy's vision? Is the story suggesting that art itself is as important as what it represents?

☐ 7   The Dance of the Star (page 48)

Origin
Indian, the classic story of the six blind people and the elephant.

Background
The original story is of six blind people, each of whom touches a single part of an elephant. Each believes on the basis of this limited experience that they now know what an elephant is like. The story is generally interpreted as being about the importance of approaching issues holistically, and of seeing a reality as a system of interdependent parts rather than as a set of unrelated fragments.

Treatment
The physical elephant in the classic story is here transformed into a metaphor for the 'good life', and therefore a person's sense of fulfilment as a human being. This is given six interpretations, each of which is partial and therefore distorted.

Reflection
How would the star have expressed the six interpretations in her dance? Would any one of the six qualities be enough for a full life? If so, which? Is it possible to rank them in any order of value? What are the disadvantages and limitations of each if pursued alone? Do the six together say all there is to say about the good life?

☐ 8   The Wandering Sheep (page 50)

Origin
Christian, evoking biblical imagery.

Background
Throughout the Bible, God is frequently likened to a good shepherd.

Treatment
The story suggests that a good shepherd may be female as well as male, and may permit — or even encourage — the sheep in her care to err and stray.

Reflection
How can you show your love if you let go? How can you show your love if you don't? What message does the parable have for parents ... teachers ... leaders ... lovers ... and friends?

☐ 9   So Near and Yet So Far (page 51)

Origin

Jewish, East European.

Background

This parable belongs to the tradition of slightly absurd tales which require some suspension of reality, and which have a strong moral or psychological message.

Treatment

The original form is retained with the addition of colour and detail, the use of dialogue, and the introduction of a female role.

Reflection

What does the dream contribute to the story? Why did it seem so likely that the treasure would be far away? What does the treasure represent?

☐ 10   Five Journeys (page 52)

Origin

Tibetan, Buddhist.

Background

There is a strong tradition of monastic education in all branches of Buddhism. A lama is a spiritual leader of the Tibetan tradition.

Treatment

In the original version, four monks are distracted from their mission by worldly temptations. In this version, the four are 'distracted' by something which is itself an element of the fifth teacher's message.

Reflection

What might the lama have meant by 'We shall be fortunate...'? — Did he mean, fortunate if at least one gets through? Or if only one gets through? On reaching the south, what might the fifth teacher say about the other four teachers and their journeys? Is the journey of the fifth teacher as important as — or more important than — the journeys of the other four?

☐ 11   The Monastery (page 53)

Origin

Modern Christian parable.

Background

According to Jewish belief, the Messiah (literally, 'anointed one') is awaited as the one who will right all wrongs and establish an age of justice, peace, harmony and love. The Messiah is usually personified, sometimes in royal, sometimes in military imagery; but also can be portrayed as an ordinary person who appears without warning, and who may mysteriously reside anywhere, and be anyone at any time.

Treatment

The original version features a rabbi, but here the Jewish character is female. This version contributes to the theme of reconciliation between Christians and Jews and, in particular, reflects the growing number of Christians who acknowledge that they have much to learn, both spiritually and morally, from Judaism.

Reflection

What is the connection between the poor quality of religious life in the monastery and the poor quality of relationships? What is the effect of making the Jewish character a woman rather than a man? What the Christians in this story gain from the Jew is obvious: what, if anything, does the Jew gain from the Christians? Are we to suppose that it was God who sent the rabbi's wife to the monastery? If so, what were the messages which God was intending to provide for Jewish people on the one hand and for Christian people on the other?

☐ 12   Give and Take (page 54)

Origin

Modern Jewish.

Background

Yom Kippur (Day of Atonement) is an annual festival which always falls in September or October. It is the culmination of a period of reflection, repentance and reconciliation, and involves a twenty-five hour period of fasting which lasts from sunset to sunset. It is customary for all observant Jews to attend synagogue on this day. There is a tradition within Judaism of arguing and bargaining with God. This is not considered to be blasphemous but, paradoxically, to be reverential.

Treatment

The original version involves a man, and mentions that he is a tailor. The treatment here provides considerably more external detail, and greater insight into the central character's inner life.

Reflection

Does the central character merely shift blame from herself to God or does she genuinely feel she has the kind of relationship with God that has a lot of give and take? Does she seriously believe that God could, or would, have prevented the disasters which she lists? Is the bargain she proposes realistic and reasonable? What might the woman behind her think that she should demand of God — and hold out for? What is the story suggesting about the nature of agreements or covenants between God and humankind, and about the nature of forgiveness?

☐ 13   No Lonely Soul (page 56)

Origin

Irish.

Background

The banshee in Irish folklore is an invisible and formless creature who is believed to be always lurking nearby, ready to pounce on anyone who misbehaves, or to snatch the soul of anyone who is lonely and unhappy.

Treatment

The imagery and reference points in this version belong to an industrial society and an urban setting. The version uses the traditional storytelling device of repeating a sequence of words at key points: paradoxically this both threatens and comforts, for it increases the suspense and yet also implies that fears and anxieties can be kept under control, and that all will be well.

Reflection

Do the people in the story believe that the banshee exists? If so, is it merely through fear of the banshee that they show love and affection, and that they comfort and protect each other? Or are there better and stronger reasons? Either way, what examples of togetherness occur here? Are they a reasonably comprehensive list? If I myself had been telling this story, which examples would I have included? If the banshee is to be understood as a symbol, or as a fantasy projected by the human imagination, what is it that she stands for?

☐ 14   The Night We Cried (page 57)

Origin

Jewish, oral testimony from the Holocaust period.

Background

Men and women in the Nazi concentration camps were generally kept entirely separate from each other. Nevertheless some members of the same family were sometimes able to stay together and this undoubtedly enabled them to survive in the deepest sense. Indeed, among the small number who survived the Holocaust, many attribute their survival to the quality of the relationships which sustained and supported them.

Treatment

The testimony is re-created here in the style of a transcript of someone recalling and reflecting on their experience.

Reflection

Why did the mother and daughter not share the soup? Why were they both so willing to lose it? How do I respond to the fact that the husband's death took place on the same day that his wife wasted the soup? What significance do the mother and daughter themselves see in this coincidence?

☐ 15   Savitri (page 58)

Origin

Hindu.

Background

Princess Savitri was an only child, born to her parents in their old age. Many royal families throughout India approached her parents for her hand in marriage, and her parents requested her to choose her own husband.

Treatment

Traditional style but with use of flash-back.

Reflection

Why doesn't Savitri explain to her husband why her heart is so heavy? Why does she insist on going with him into the forest? Do I see her assertiveness with Yama as surprising, or is it the fruit of her three days of prayer and fasting? Is she justified in using a trick in order to save her husband's life? Why does the storyteller refer at the end to the birds of the forest and the family of monkeys?

☐ 16   Return to the Sky (page 60)

Origin

Zulu.

Background

Cattle are a major aspect of wealth in many traditional African societies. A calabash is a hollow gourd used as a container, especially for food or liquids. Women take pride in the baskets they weave and exchange.

Treatment

Conventional , with heightened sensuality.

Reflection

Does she really hope that he will try to discover her secret and that she will then be free to return? Should she have a secret from her husband? Does he have secrets from her? What does it mean that she has come from the sky? Why is the basket significant as the symbol of a secret place? If she knows her secret is invisible and that he will never be able to discover it, why does she pretend to hide it in a basket? Is his love for her genuine, or is he selfish and possessive?

☐ 17 Recipe for a Happy Marriage (page 62)

Origin

Kerala, South India.

Treatment

A traditional pre-industrial tale is told here with the sensationalism and narrative conventions of a modern tabloid newspaper: overlapping flashbacks, irrelevant detail, quotations lifted from context, and so on.

Background

The extended family in Indian village life places emphasis both on 'horizontal' and 'vertical' relationships. A key element is the domestic legacy of secret or distinctive recipes which bond together the female members of the family. Much life is lived in the open, and the shared courtyards are arenas for the exchange of news and advice.

Reflection

How can I explain the behaviour of the husband to his wife? How can I explain the behaviour of the wife to her husband? Does she really forgive him or does she accept that as a woman she has no choice but to be the victim of violence by men? Where does she get her strength? What is the effect of recasting a traditional tale in the genre of a tabloid newspaper? Does it imply that there are common experiences, concerns and values in different places and in different periods? Does a happy marriage have a secret ingredient? If so, what does this story suggest it might be?

☐ 18 The Match (page 64)

Origin

Jewish.

Treatment

Conventional narration, and conventional use of three elements — with a 'twist' on the third — but with contemporary reference to a dating agency.

Background

The story reflects an affectionately mocking attitude towards 'philosophy' and belongs to that genre of Jewish literature which affirms the importance of something, in this case philosophy and a young person's search for a partner, by poking fun at it. Food and family appear in many Jewish stories as symbols of continuity and connection.

Reflection

Why do I think the matchmaker chose those three subjects as icebreakers? What subjects would I myself recommend in a similar situation? How does the matchmaker probably imagine the conversation would go? In what ways is philosophy different from food and family? Does the young woman really understand what philosophy is about? How might the young man respond to her last question? Does she reach him? How important is discussion of 'philosophy' in close relationships?

☐ 19 Gifts (page 65)

Origin

Muslim, from the Palestinian region during the Ottoman empire.

Background

Hajj — setting out with a definite purpose — is the pilgrimage to Makka and a duty which devout Muslims joyfully undertake at least once in their lifetime. Hajj itself lasts about 10 days but the journey to and from Makka may take months or years, depending on the distance and the mode of travel. For those who are unable to go on hajj, greeting a returning hajji is a blessing. 'Souvenirs' are always well received.

Treatment

Conventional, with traces of stream of consciousness.

Reflection

What gifts did the hajji bring his wife and children? What gifts did they have for him? Why was the husband away so long? Has he put religious observance above family life? When he sees the third child, does he assume that his wife has been unfaithful to him? Do I also assume this? Or do I have another explanation? What is his wife trying to tell him? Why does she choose to break off and attend to the baby rather than finish what she is saying? What effect might the existence of the fourth child have on the husband's understanding of the situation?

☐ 20 Slender Threads (page 66)

Origin

Celtic Christian.

Background

Stories such as this date from Europe in the 8th and 9th centuries of the Christian era. There was a strong tradition in Celtic monasticism of rejoicing in the natural world and of seeing God in all creation. Commitment to God necessarily involved stewardship of the earth. The story echoes the Christian values of forgiveness, self-sacrifice and loving one's enemy, and uses language from the Eucharist and from Celtic devotional writings.

Treatment

Two separate legends about Kevin have been woven together here: the bird building a nest in the hermit's hand has been set in the context of the story about the cow and the herdsman. The story is told through the eyes of the cow, though this is not made immediately explicit.

Reflection

As I learned of the narrator's feelings for Kevin, how did I react, and why? Why is the story told by the cow? At what stage did I realise who the narrator was? Did that in any way alter my reaction to their relationship? Did I feel pleasure, disgust, envy, confusion, indifference, fascination.......? Was I annoyed that I assumed at first that the narrator was a woman? What was there about Kevin that attracted her? How do we understand the herd's illness — and their later wholeness? What does the building of the nest tell us about the nature of prayer and scriptural study? What spiritual and moral insights are offered through the imagery of slender threads?

☐ 21 Speaking to the Emperor (page 68)

Origin
Sikh.

Background
There were ten Sikh gurus. They were teachers, and were honoured in the Sikh community for their message, and their moral and spiritual example. The Sikh tradition has experienced much antagonism and even opposition since its emergence in the 15th century. Many stories of the gurus are concerned with the need for moral and spiritual resistance to oppression, and proclaim a vision of justice and unity. Guru Hargobind (1595 — 1645 CE), the son of Guru Arjan, was the sixth guru and enjoyed an ambivalent relationship with the Mogul rulers in India at that time.

Treatment
Traditional, but involving a series of flashbacks, and the recollection of some sayings of Guru Arjan.

Reflection
Why have so many people gathered at the prison? Why does it seem to be such a momentous occasion? What might Guru Hargobind mean by fighting fears inside the human heart and mind? Why was the Emperor persuaded that divine aid might make him well if he imprisoned a holy man who would pray for his recovery? Was the Emperor's action justified? How do the three sayings from Guru Arjan throw light on this story? What do I think Guru Hargobind does when he leaves the prison? What will he say or ask in his prayers? What will he say to the Emperor?

☐ 22 A Shady Deal (page 70)

Origin
Uygar people in Xinjiang, north west China; this story is found in many versions throughout the East.

Background
The Effendi (or Effendi Nasrudin) is a legendary hero, noted for his wit, his passion for justice, his resourcefulness, and his lateral thinking.

Treatment
Modernised with freshly created realia (notices, documents, headlines and song).

Reflection
Can any one individual own a tree, or do trees belong to the whole community, or do trees belong to no one at all? Do wealthy people have the right to keep what they own to themselves? Do they have any responsibility to share it with others? Why do the people choose the Effendi to spearhead their campaign? What do the people and the Effendi have that the landowner lacks? Is the Effendi justified in tricking the landowner? Does he 'make the tyrant look a fool'? What is likely to be the response to the 'For Sale' sign? Has the Effendi been successful?

☐ 23 The Football Match (page 73)

Origin

Christian.

Background

Religions come into conflict with each other because they make competing truth claims, but also because they are used by people who are in disputes with each other over territory, resources, freedom and power: participants in a conflict frequently hold that 'God is on their side' in order to raise their own morale and sense of righteousness rather than because they are genuinely religious. On the surface, sport provides a light-hearted metaphor for this opposition, but there are serious undercurrents of hostility — both during and after the game of life.

Treatment

The original version features Catholics and Protestants. The treatment here presents Christians and Muslims, and offers a model for examining interfaith and inter-ethnic relations on a wide scale in the modern world. The metaphorical nature of this treatment is important to stress because while the personification of God is central to Christianity, it is inimical to Islam. In Christian devotion and teachings it is believed that God became human in the person of Jesus Christ; for Muslims, however, God can never take any physical form. God in the original version is male; here, God is presented as female.

Reflection

What might it mean that God 'came down from heaven'? Why does God dress herself like the supporters? Why might God support each side in turn? Why do both sides think God is completely mad, and why don't they do anything to her? Why does their attention in the arcade focus on God rather than on each other, or on the match between them? What is the game now? What is God 'playing at'? How is this match an image of 'the game of life'? Why does the storyteller choose to make God female?

☐ 24 Two Kinds of Idiot (page 74)

Origin

Indian folktale from the Madya Pradesh region.

Background

The original involves a young wife who is approached at a well by four travellers who ask, in turn, for water. She asks them riddles which they cannot answer and then takes them to her home. She is rebuked by her father-in-law for bringing strangers to the house when there is no one else there, and is reported to the king. She explains the riddles to the king, who admires her wit and quick thinking.

Treatment

Transposed from an Indian village to a Western city; from a village well to a municipal park; and from a home to an office block.

Reflection

What do I understand by 'homeless', 'drop-out', 'poor and oppressed', 'idiot'? Do I have a 'third' for each of these? Are the secretary's examples adequate? Why does the secretary not explain her actions to her boss as fully as she does to the personnel manager? Why does she mention the firm's charitable donations, social responsibility policies and third world concerns? Does this strengthen her case? Is she right to interpret these values in the particular way that she does? What happened to the four young men?

☐ 25 Draupadi's Prayer (page 76)

Origin

Hindu, from the epic collection of tales known as *The Mahabharata.*

Background

In the Hindu tradition, God has creating, destroying and renewing aspects. For many Hindus, God takes a variety of forms, though individual Hindus and Hindu communities are likely to be devoted to one of these incarnations in particular. Lord Krishna is especially adored as a baby, and as a young man; stories of Krishna show his power to conquer evil and to restore purity. The quotation from Krishna in this story is from the *Bhagavad Gita.*

Treatment

Traditional, with reference to a saying by Krishna.

Reflection

What is Yuddhishthira gambling when he uses Draupadi as a stake? How does losing possessions compare with losing a beloved partner in a game? Why is Duryodhana especially pleased to 'win' Draupadi? Is it a sign of weakness or of strength in Draupadi that she realises that she is helpless, and that no one but Lord Krishna can save her? When she lets go of her covering, is she too gambling? What does it mean that the miracle happens when Draupadi lets go of her covering? How do I understand the extending of her sari? In what ways is prayer a gamble? In what ways is life a gamble?

☐ 26 The Door (page 77)

Origin

Zen Buddhist.

Background

A feature of Zen is the sudden flash of inspiration which happens suddenly in the context of an apparently eventless period of meditation or an undifferentiated sequence of events in everyday life.

Treatment

Conventional.

Reflection

What might have been unfair, and how was she being treated? How else might she have chosen to right the wrong? What does she expect the king to do? Is it worth staying at the door so long? Does she change over the years, and if so in what ways, and why? What makes people ask her advice? What might they ask advice about? What advice does she give them? Is it worth waiting so long for her advice? Why, at the end, did she not move? Has she perhaps forgotten why she came to the door in the first place, or does it no longer matter? Why does the door close? Is there a door at which I stand?

☐ 27 In the Bag (page 78)

Origin

North African Christian.

Background

Stories of magic bags (or other vessels) capable of absorbing evil abound in the folklore of Europe and the Middle East. Belief in life after death is strongly developed in the Christian tradition, and heaven and hell as places or states of reward and punishment have reality for many Christians. In some communities elements of Christian belief exist alongside earlier beliefs and superstitions.

Treatment

Traditional.

Reflection

What do the priests mean by saying that you can only get to heaven by going to church? Is this reasonable? What does it mean that the magician's bag swallows evil? And that it swallows the priests? Why does the last priest behave differently? Is he sincere or shrewd? Is the swallowing up of hell a courageous or a cowardly action? Why would the receptionist be afraid if the magician's bag swallowed up heaven? How would that solve the magician's problem? Who was 'a certain priest' and why was there a twinkle in his eye? What would I like to swallow up?

☐ 28 The Stonecutter (page 79)

Origin

China, Tao tradition.

Background

There is a strong tradition in Tao philosophy of acceptance and creative passivity, as distinct from aggressive activity arising from a desire to change and to control events and situations.

Treatment

Conventional narrative style, with traditional use of repetition.

Reflection

What is it in his own everyday work that the stonecutter finds unsatisfying? In what similar ways are other people's lives unsatisfying? What is it he is really looking for? What does he come to realise at the end about the potential of a stonecutter's work? What are the implications of the story for people such as myself?

□ 29 Means and Ends (page 80)

Origin

Modern Jewish.

Background

There is a strong emphasis in many religious traditions that God meets human need through service undertaken by human beings to their neighbours rather than through a 'miraculous' intervention which would involve changing or suspending natural and scientific laws. Particularly in Judaism there is a tradition of complaining against, or remonstrating with, God — as seen also, for example, in the story in this book entitled *Give and Take*.

Treatment

Conventional narrative style, though with use at one point of a cinematic 'jump-cut'.

Reflection

Where and how did the family form the belief that God would intervene miraculously to save them? Were the people in the cart, the boat and the helicopter religious believers, and did they think of themselves as having been sent by God? What would I myself have replied to the family, if I had been in the cart, the boat or the helicopter? Is the family right to remonstrate with God at the end? What might they reply or do in the light of what God says?

□ 30 Just the Ticket (page 81)

Origin

Modern Jewish.

Background

Many religious traditions emphasise the importance of human responsibility and stewardship, and warn against resignation and fatalism and trusting merely in good luck. The idea of an agreement or covenant between God and humankind is particularly important in Judaism.

Treatment

Conventional narrative style, but with God portrayed as using slangy business language, as if doing a deal in the marketplace, rather than the literary or high-flown language which is customary in religious writings.

Reflection

Would someone really believe that they could win a lottery without buying a ticket? If so, what else might they believe? In what ways, if any, am I myself prone to behave and think like the main character in this story? Do I believe that there is a God who both would and could arrange for a particular ticket in a lottery to be drawn? If not, what is the real meaning of the words attributed to God at the end of the story — 'meet me half way'?

☐ 31 God Willing (page 82)

Origin
Christian, and versions exist also in Judaism and Islam.

Background
The story reflects religious teachings that human beings should develop and use their talents, skills and initiative, and should not shelter behind religious faith as a substitute for this.

Treatment
The original version is usually about a holy man and a tailor. It is transposed here to a modern setting (for example through the reference to the minibus), and the main character is female.

Reflection
What beliefs about God and religion do I imagine the mechanic probably has? And what are his views of women? Where did he perhaps get these ideas and views from? What does the Mother Superior assume about him? What might his reaction be to her final message? Will her message cause him to change any of his views? If so, which?

☐ 32 Say No More (page 83)

Origin
Modern, but with imagery and assumptions drawn from traditional Arabian folklore.

Background
A jinn (also sometimes known as a djinn, jinnee or genie) is a spirit in Arabian folklore which is able to appear in human or animal form, and is able either to help or to hinder human beings. Often in popular mythology jinns are imagined to reside within receptacles such as lamps or vases. In the *Arabian Nights*, Aladdin is famously able to summon a jinn to his assistance by rubbing a magic lamp.

Treatment
Conventional narrative style, with two separate uses of repetition. The one repetitive sequence gives the story an up-to-date and yuppie-style setting, whilst the other evokes a pre-industrial village community. This juxtaposition suggests that the story's message is universal.

Reflection
Does the man's fiancee know that he is approaching the wise woman of the village for help? Do members of his family know? Does he genuinely expect that she will help him in the way he requests? If so, what gave him the idea that she can provide such assistance? Does she know what the jinn will say to him? If so, why doesn't she save him the trouble of consulting the jinn directly? What is it she is trying to teach him? What kind of help could the jinn perhaps give?

☐ 33   A Double Life (page 84)

Origin

Jewish, from a Jewish community in Eastern Europe in the 18th century.

Background

The story reflects Jewish teachings about religious leadership and about the importance of humanitarian service to one's fellow human beings. For over 1000 years the heartland of Jewish culture was in Eastern Europe, and was nurtured and developed within the context of closely-knit communities. The basic theme here, of a secular Jew from a cosmopolitan and pluralist city visiting an observant Jewish village community, and discovering or redis-covering religious faith there, is a frequent motif in East European Judaism.

Treatment

Conventional narrative style.

Reflection

What are the assumptions of the visitor at the start of the story, for example about the appropriate behaviour of rabbis? Where did he get these from? Why do the members of the community not explain to him entirely directly and explicitly where the rabbi is? Why doesn't he question the rabbi directly? Was he wrong to spy on the rabbi? Would it have been better if he had simply talked with the rabbi? If not, why not?

☐ 34   I'm Staying Here (page 86)

Origin

Tao and Buddhist, and versions exist also in Christianity.

Background

Stillness, self-examination and contemplation are highly valued in all religious traditions.

Treatment

Conventional narrative style, but the story is more usually about three male characters rather than, as here, about three women. The reference to involvement in politics, and the use of the modern term 'burnt-out', imply a contemporary setting.

Reflection

What other things might the first two sisters have left home to do? Would they have found these similarly unsatisfying? What experi-ences in her childhood and growing up has the third sister had which cause her to be different from the two others? Why does she use the muddy water to make her point? Could she have made her point just as easily with words alone? Will the two sisters leave home again in due course? Do I hope that they will?

☐ 35 The Way to Go (page 87)

Origin
Modern Buddhist.

Background
In Buddhism, as in all religious traditions, there is emphasis on the need for balance between worship and work, and between meeting spiritual and material needs. Siddhartha Gautama Buddha, the founder of Buddhism referred to in this story, died in about 480 BCE. Countries where this story might be set include India, Myanmar (formerly Burma), Nepal, Sri Lanka, Tibet and Vietnam.

Treatment
Conventional narrative style.

Reflection
Which do the villagers need more, a road or a temple? What are the advantages and disadvantages of each? What questions would I put to them if they asked my advice on this? In what ways are a temple and a road similar to each other? What does the monk mean at the end — that he is not going to build a temple after all, or not yet, or that it is going to be a particular kind of temple, or built in a particular kind of way?

☐ 36 Calm in a Teacup (page 88)

Origin
Modern Jewish.

Background
Philosophers sometimes use an image drawn from everyday life to encapsulate life itself.

Treatment
The original version refers to a glass of wine, not a cup of tea.

Reflection
Who might the two characters be? Where are they, and what has brought them together? Why are they staring into their cups? Why does one of them speak finally? Why does life have to be 'like' something? Is it reasonable for the second one to expect the first to explain what was meant? Why doesn't the first explain? Would a philosopher be able to explain? What is a philosopher? Am I a philosopher? What is life 'like' for me?

☐ 37   Is There Anybody There? (page 89)

Origin
Modern Jewish.

Background
The story has in common with many religious stories that it invites reflection on the difference between mature faith on the one hand and simplistic belief in divine intervention on the other.

Treatment
Conventional.

Reflection
What response does the man on the edge of the cliff expect? Who or what responds to him? Why does he feel unable to comply ? What does he mean by 'anybody else'?

☐ 38   Paradise Gardens (page 90)

Origin
Arab folktale, within the Islamic tradition.

Background
Adam is the first of the prophets in the Islamic tradition and the prototype of humanity. The world of Islamic folklore sometimes offers possibilities of 'flight' to other places and states of consciousness. Angels are messengers from God.

Treatment
In the original version the main character is a woodcutter, and he wishes to dig up the bones of 'old father Adam'. The setting here has been modernised, for example by making the main character a civil servant and by having him transported to a theme park instead of the Garden of Eden.

Reflection
What are the aspects of modern life in the Western world which create or increase feelings of irrelevance and impersonality? How can Adam's disobedience and punishment possibly explain why human beings have to slave away at pointless chores? Why does the angel arranged for the civil servant to go to a theme park? Why is it called Paradise Gardens? Why do I suppose the angel tells the civil servant not to ask questions in the park? What are angels and how else might angels be disguised? How are we to understand the three experiences which the civil servant has in the park? At the end of the story, has the civil servant changed at all and, if so, how?

☐ 39 Standing Up and Sitting Down (page 92)

Origin
Yoruba (West African) traditional folktale.

Background
In Yoruba culture the king relies for advice on a number of elders who are respected by all members of the community for their experience and wisdom. Typically, these elders are indeed elderly.

Treatment
Fairly traditional, with emphasis on the standing and sitting motif.

Reflection
How does the king's self-image develop in this story? In what senses are 'standing' and 'sitting' used? What qualities make for a good elder, that is, an adviser to someone in power? Were the young men right to expect that their positions would be secure after they had killed their fathers? Did the young man know how the king would react to his 'riddle' or was he taking a huge risk? What happened to the rest of the young men in the end?

☐ 40 The Needle (page 94)

Origin
Sikh

Background
Guru Nanak (1469–1539 CE) was the first of the ten Sikh gurus (religious teachers). An important element in his preaching was the need for religious men and women to live an active life within the community, and to devote themselves to issues of justice and equality. Lahore, which is now part of Pakistan, was once the major city of the region of India called Punjab. The Sikh tradition was born in the Punjab.

Treatment
Traditional material is expanded with details of a banquet, and the story is rendered in the form of a letter.

Reflection
Do sudden changes usually last? Why did the guru use a physical object to make his point? Why that object? Why was it easier for Dudi Chand's wife to see the point Guru Nanak was making? Was the point better received by Dudi Chand because it was made by a guru? In what ways did Dudi Chand and his wife use their wealth to help the poor? Why is it important for them to be remembered? Why might Guru Nanak find that they will be happier? In what ways might they have changed for the better?

☐ 41   Last Things (page 96)

Origin
Jewish.

Background
The dying man has not written a last will and testament, and it is likely that his estate will therefore go to his widow. On his deathbed he indicates how he would like some of his possessions distributed to his children.

Treatment
Transposed to a contemporary and wealthy British setting.

Reflection
Should the wishes of the dead always be honoured? Why is it important to so many people to have something which belonged to the dead, in order to remember them? Why does this dying man want his children to have something of his? If he does die, will the widow respect his wishes? Did focusing on his likely death prevent him from hoping that he would recover? Did it help him to have a more peaceful death? What else might the couple have discussed?

☐ 42   The Precious Stone (page 97)

Origin
Indian.

Background
The wandering holy man — a 'sannyasi' — is a classical feature of Hindu tradition. He represents one of the four stages of life, and is a person who has given up worldly wealth, concerns and ambitions in order to devote his time to meditation and contemplation. Not all Hindus aspire to this stage and way of life, and there are some who reach it while still young.

Treatment
Traditional, but with the use of repetition to provide additional texture.

Reflection
How can people fulfil themselves outside the world? How can people fulfil themselves within it? Why was the businessman troubled? In the end, had the holy man given the businessman a priceless stone and made him 'rich for ever'? How did he do this?

☐ **43 That Dying Feeling (page 98)**

Origin
East European folktale.

Background
The wizened figure is a personification of death.

Treatment
The original version features a young man and a series of old men. The treatment here gives insight into the central character's longing for 'eternal' life and the nature of the mortal world. It also generates images of infinity and finitude.

Reflection
In what other ways do people experience 'that dying feeling' while they are still alive? In what sense might it be similar to the experience of death? How can we understand the journey the young woman makes and the places she passes — where and what are they? Is it true that the mountain will not turn to dust until the sun no longer warms the earth? Are the sun and the mountain long-lasting rather than everlasting? Why does the young woman settle for life on the mountain? Should no one ever go back to the life they left behind? In her situation, would I have ignored the old woman's advice and got down to help the wizened creature? Would it be worth it and would death catch up with me in the end anyway? Is eternal life possible after death — rather than before or instead of death?

☐ **44 Out of Fright, out of Mind (page 100)**

Origin
Muslim, Sufi.

Background
In many traditions, sea and ships are images of life and people's journey through it.

Treatment
The original version features a pasha and a philosopher. The treatment here involves seafaring language and imagery.

Reflection
Why are the sea and ships so often used as images of life? Why might this man be going to sea for the first time? Would anything else have made him calmer, since comfort and insults don't work? Why do they throw him overboard? Why do they haul him back in? Does it 'do the trick'? If I were in an extreme moment, and my whole life passed before me, what would I see?

☐ 45 A Handful of Soil (page 101)

Origin

Christian.

Background

Crete is an island in the Eastern Mediterranean, off the mainland of Greece. There has been a Christian presence on the island for almost 2000 years, and most inhabitants are of the Greek Orthodox tradition. For some Christians heaven is a 'place' where good people go after death; for many it is a state — imagined as a place — of eternal happiness.

Treatment

Traditional, with traditional use of repetition in a three-part motif.

Reflection

What is significant about Petros sitting at his door? Why does he want to take soil from Crete with him? How might he imagine that God would collect him? Why does God come in disguises? Why is Petros not allowed to bring the soil with him? Why does he refuse to let go of the soil? What is it about his great-grand-daughter that enables him to open his fist and let go of the soil? What does it mean that he sees Crete in heaven? What would I clench in my fist? Who or what would I let go of it for? What do I want to see in heaven?

☐ 46 In Search of a Cure (page 102)

Origin

Buddhist.

Background

Buddhist teaching is based on the impermanence of life and the danger of illusions. Siddhartha Gautama Buddha died in about 480 BCE. Countries where this story might be set include India, Myanmar (formerly Burma), Nepal, Sri Lanka, Tibet and Vietnam.

Treatment

Modernised, with additional details.

Reflection

Why was the mother of the dead child seeking help? What help and wholeness did she need? What did I imagine the Buddha would do with any grains which she collected? Would that mission enable me to knock on strangers' doors? Can we ever understand what someone else has experienced or appreciate what they might be feeling? How do similar experiences and emotions link with us? How might different experiences and emotions link us? Did she find help and wholeness?

☐ 47 The Bird, the Forest and the Cage (page 103)

Origin

Muslim, attributed to Rumi.

Background

Belief in the afterlife is central to Islamic theology.

Treatment

Fairly close to the original, with dialogue added. Arranged in four sections for sequencing exercises.

Reflection

Why does the businessman deliver the message from the caged bird to the forest birds? Why doesn't he realise this is a message to himself, and why doesn't he release her? Why do the birds not dare to speak? What might they have said? Do birds love as humans love? What makes the caged bird drop dead? What enables her to fly again? Were her freedom and her new life planned? By whom? How is freedom gained by dying? Does all death lead to freedom? Where is the caged bird's lover now? How can she fly to him?

☐ 48 Hanging on for Life (page 104)

Origin

Jewish, based on oral testimony from the Holocaust.

Background

Most Jewish survivors of the Holocaust feel a powerful urge to tell their story, in order that names may not be forgotten, and that beauty, dignity and purity may shine out from that evil period. They also need to understand how and why they themselves survived, when so many others perished.

Treatment

Close to the original testimony, with some insights offered into the behaviour of the Nazis, and into the thought processes of the victims.

Reflection

Why do the victims not comment on the behaviour of their oppressors? Does the narrator — a survivor of that experience — comment on it directly or indirectly? Why did the Nazi guards want the camp inmates to choose or, at least, to seem to choose? Was it better for the inmates if they had a choice, or the appearance of choice? Is the most painful decision how to die? What does it mean to die with dignity? Is it more important than staying alive? How can we choose between our physical survival, individually or collectively, and our moral survival? Why might the narrator have become sceptical about religion and what had he rejected that the rabbi represented? What draws him and the rabbi together? Is the rabbi right to see goodness — and potential — in everything? Is everything 'in the will of God'? What does the pit represent — and the other side? What does it mean to hang on?

☐ 49   Daring to Fly (page 106)

Origin

Black American.

Background

Black American consciousness is shaped by the historic experience of slavery, by the continuing experience of racism, and by the community's responses to these experiences. Chronicles by white Americans of the period of slavery depicted a largely passive black slave population which was eventually emancipated by white liberals. Attempts at self-emancipation were difficult and dangerous, and successes were mostly unreported or suppressed by the whites who shaped national history and controlled contemporary public media. Nevertheless there exists an extensive oral tradition which celebrates a range of physical, moral and spiritual acts of resistance, and which can contribute to the redemption from slavery for black and white people together.

Treatment

Traditional, with echoes near the start of a poem by the black American poet Margaret Walker. The characters have been given names which recall significant figures in the Israelite exodus recorded in the bible — a story which resonates with many black slaves and their ancestors, as it does with Jews.

Reflection

Why is it important to us to know the circumstances of our birth? How does Miriam feel about her own baby? What would she tell him about the circumstances of his birth? Why does the narrator say that the sun beating down on America is the same sun that beat down on Africa? What do I think Moses means when he first tells Miriam to dare to fly? In what way is Miriam 'the mother of them all'? Why does Moses wait for a serious injury or insult to break a slave before he tells them that they can fly? Where is home for these slaves? Where is home for me? What new life will they give birth to — and how? How do I understand the people flying? How do the overseer and slave owner understand it? Is the telling of the story part of the flying? Is the listening to it? Do I dare fly?

☐ 50   Whoever Comes This Way (page 108)

Origin

African, Zimbabwe region.

Background

Colonialism has shaped the self-concept of many peoples. Parallels with inequalities of power in the animal world serve to explore layers of cultural and political oppression in human affairs, and physical and economic exploitation.

Treatment

A specific gender dimension — and potential for interpretation — has been introduced through the designation of the lion as male and the tortoise as female. Dialogue with recurring refrains has been added to the original version to heighten the dramatic effect.

Reflection

How can we understand the permanent effect on the land which the tortoise's actions, such as scratching, seemed to have? Would the tortoise have been better advised to attack the lion and hope to overpower him? Would that have been a real struggle? Should she have acquiesced altogether? Would that have been more dignified? Why does she repeat her first words to the lion? How and why does she struggle to the end?

7
Thereby Hangs a Tale

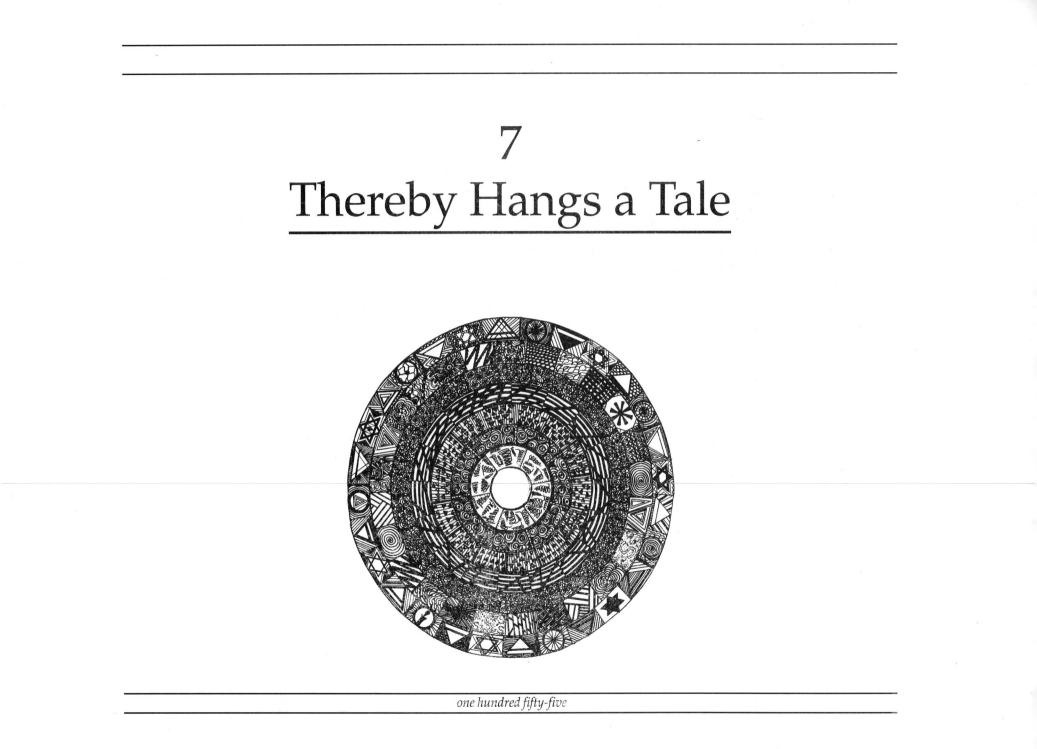

Index of Traditions

Index of Titles

8
To Be Continued

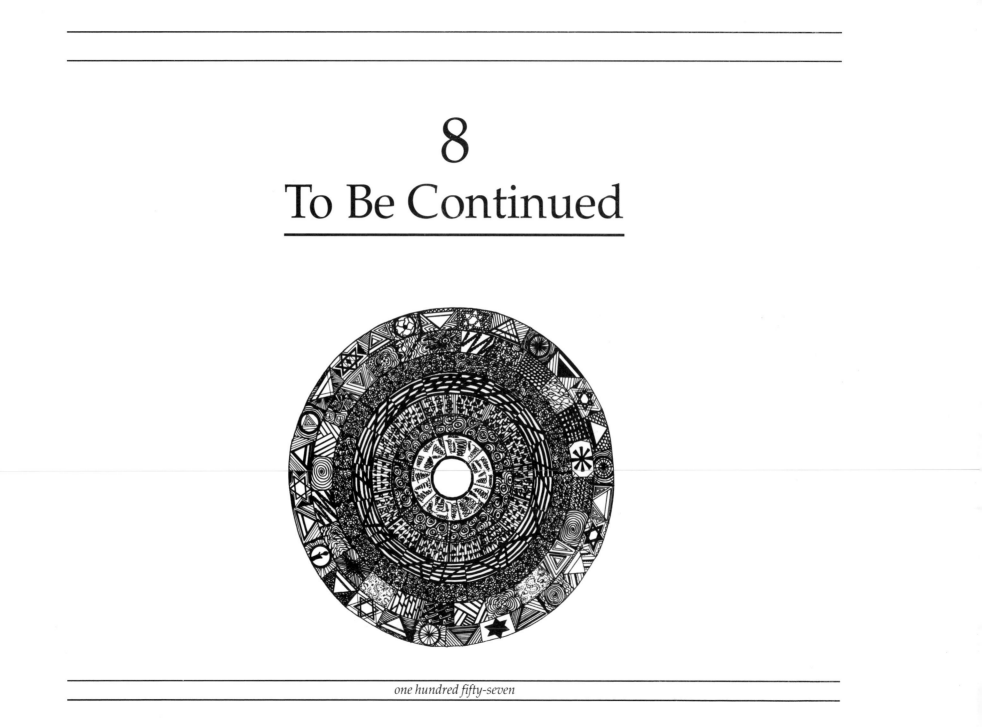

Whilst compiling this book we have had occasion to consult, and draw ideas from, the following works:

Anon: *The Gold Plant and Other Tales of the Effendi*, Beijing: Foreign Languages Press, 1986.

Bausch, William J: *Storytelling, Imagination and Faith*, Mystic, Connecticut: Twenty Third Publications, 1984.

Bushnaq, Inea: *Arab Folk Tales*, London: Penguin, 1986.

Chaudhury, P C Roy: *Best Loved Folk Tales of India*, London: Oriental University Press, 1987.

de Mello, Anthony: *The Song of the Bird*, New York: Image Books, 1984.

de Mello, Anthony: *One Minute Wisdom*, Anand India: Gujarat Sahitys Prakash, 1985.

Eliach, Yaffa: *Hasidic Tales of the Holocaust*, New York: Avon Books, 1982.

Gbadamosi, Bukare and Beier, Ulli: *Not Even God is Ripe Enough: Yoruba Tales*, London: Heinemann 1968.

Hamilton, Virginia: *The People Could Fly: American Black Folktales*, London: Walker Books, 1986.

Hoff, Benjamin: *The Tao of Pooh*, London: Methuen, 1982.

Kanawa, Kiri Te: *Land of the Long White Cloud: Maori myths, tales and legends*, London: Pavilion Books, 1989.

Lefever, Henry: *One Man and His Dog*, London: Lutterworth, 1973.

Merton, Thomas: *The Wisdom of the Desert*, London: Sheldon Press, 1961.

Narayan, R K: *Gods, Demons and Others*, New Delhi: Vision Books, 1987.

Shah, Idries: *Thinkers of the East*, London: Penguin, 1971.

Shah, Idries: *World Tales*, London and New York: Harcourt Brace Jovanovich, 1979.

Singh, Rani and Jugnu: *Stories from the Sikh World*, London: Macdonald, 1987.

Van de Weyer, Robert: *Celtic Fire*, London: Darton, Longman and Todd, 1991.